THE INVINSIBLE FINGER IN A FREE MARKET SOCIETY

Aim at corporate dishonesty

How the little guy is getting screwed By large corporations

Written by

Mark Charles Brown

The Big Dog was sleeping

CHAPTER SEVEN- Governmental Deceptions 211
Financial Bailouts of countries

Bernanke's critics of US monetary policy

Federal Reserve and the US Treasury explained

Dead Reckoning
Globalization-Did it work?

INTRODUCTION

So, this is Christmas and a full year has gone, high gas prices are back and I'm pissed off
and I'm not the only one.
We like to believe supply and demand dictates commodity prices but every year at Christmas and in the summer holidays, gas at the pump goes up substantially prior to the holidays based on of the anticipated increase in demand, not shortness of supply. So, there goes the first economic principle out the window. Demand and supply don't dictate prices, we follow the dictators.
We are definitively hijacked by gas prices because we certainly don't have any choices. We will have a choice when we buy fully electric automobiles in a few years, but for now we only have a choice of hybrid cars. But in a giving year, before Christmas, we can't trade in our automobile at the spur of the moment just in spite.
If we ask people in the business the question, ''why''? They will answer that gas retail prices reflect the international crude oil market. So, what they are trying to say is that crude oil is going up every time before Christmas and every summer? Since Saudi Arabia is the largest producer and supplier of oil, THEY are the ones turning off the wheel of supply so that we can open our wallets a little more? If that would be the answer, it would be an overly simplified answer and it is surely not the case.

Unfortunately, there are many types of oil, many players, many intermediates in the industry and everyone wants his piece of the profits. It is simple to blame someone else for gas price hikes by pointing the finger. It could be the production cost, the transportation by tankers, the brokerage cost, the refineries transformation cost, labour cost, distribution cost, more transportation cost of the final product and so on. There are many intervenient in this game than I've just mentioned because Saudi Arabia is not the only producer in the first place and they are many other countries participating in the quenching our relentless automobiles thirst. One reason why OPEC exists is to make sure all the Middle East countries are on the same page to maximize profits.

If my memory serves me right, I remember that there was an article called and a book: The Seven Sisters published in the seventies declaring that the major US oil companies were colliding to sustain high prices and were indicted by the courts of infringing the anti-Trust law and paid a fine for its misconduct. More on this later. More recently in the province of Quebec, Canada, (2010) the coalition of thirty or so retailers were indicted as well for a coalition of price fixing.

Even the retailers are there to get you if the ''bigger boys'' don't get you first.

Meaningless to say that the industry is quite complex with intertwine world players and consumers but that is what makes it intriguing. At this time of writing, I wonder if a layman such as myself can by digging information on the WWW can discover how the industry really works and who is responsible in the long line of players for giving us the FINGER?

Methodology of research; I won't do interviews or visit plants and warehouses and count tankers, only already published figures and the source will be revealed as a footnote . Information on the industry is quite overwhelming from associations to governments to specialized magazines and industry letters, banks and brokerage house analysts, newswires reporting etc., but it would be naïve of me not only to depend on the accuracy of the information but the information that is keep secret from the world. Like the daily news in the newspapers and on TV, represents only the tip of the iceberg of the truth, or should I say, a small percentage *of the relevant facts*. Most information is behind closed doors.

I often use Wikipedia Encyclopedia because of its free access and format. It is created and edited by anyone who is knowledgeable about the subject and wish to contribute. For that reason, I'm not a 100% sure of the accuracy of all the details but they can be verified with other encyclopaedias, like the Encyclopedia Britannica if needed.

For my present use and depth and objective of this book, there is more information than I need on Wikipedia Encyclopedia.

As a frustrated consumer and retiree living on a fixed income, I am obligated to consume more expensive products which seem to rise at the moment I turn my back. Cereals are also a bit of mystery, since up in Canada, we have been called "the granary of the world" but again, international prices seems to dictate the game, not the farmers or the supply. There was a 25% rise in cereal prices in general in the past two years which keeps me away from my favorite granola cereals.

This is the voyage, the journey I'm taking you to see if we are the subjects or victims as consumers of international companies controlling every aspect of our consumption and freely gauging the public whenever there is an opportunity for them.

It is with candid knowledge and limited skills and understanding that I will try to reveal the complexity of international markets, *its invisible hand and the invisible finger*.

CHAPTER ONE

Corporate   Manufacturing Deceptions

The Corporation

The ''Corporation'' has been in existence for quite a while but
the recent critics of the
The Corporation is ''too powerful'' didn't begin with the
globalization either. The power of
one is measured with Governments and the workers-the
Unions. Like a piston engine, when if
one piston goes up the other two must come down.

The Corporation has always been the object of critics since its
inception and has evolved
through time adding more power in each and every decade
through laws and fiscal policies.

The corporation is a legal entity created by the Government
which gives it the power to
execute the mandate or the mission it is designed for and being
pro-profit. Its mission is to

fabricate a product or render a service under its identity by the people who administer it for
its shareholders and hopefully making a profit at the end of the year; the reward for the venture.

Even in the 30's President Roosevelt wanted a New Deal, putting new regulations on
Corporations after seeing that GM, an American company through a subsidiary was
manufacturing war vehicles for the Germans and IBM was fabricating punch card system for
the German army. Many powerful people wanted to get rid of T. Roosevelt and let the
Corporations free by making a profit wherever they see fit.

This is the ''zone of combat'', profits at any cost without interference. Still today, some think
Government regulations don't go far enough taking in view of the recent financial scandals
or breakdowns we just suffered in 2009. Enron did not only break its own company and
brought to pauperism its employees and shareholders, it gave the reputation that
''Corporations'' were something to be afraid of, not trustworthy and dishonest and capable of
the worst crimes for profits.

Being at the heart of the capitalist system, the free enterprise system, the Corporation in itself
is not democratic. It is run by a board of directors, management and orders are
transferred down the line right through the shipping. Democracy starts at the bottom not at the
top.

Shareholders have a vote once a year and frankly, they don't even know what is going on.
The bottom line dictates their satisfaction level about management's performance.

A company is bigger than the sum of its parts. It has an image towards the public, (brand) it
has a reputation, it has influence, it has an effect on society (trends-fashion) and is embedded in
the social network and share civic responsibilities. All these cannot be found in the charter of
the company nor on the balance sheet. But they really do exist.

It is a political debate to see how far a government can regulate a company until it is called
a Socialist Government or even a Communist Government. Hard core capitalist finds
Governments too intrusive in their daily lives. For some, just sharing water sewers is Communism.

Isn't it to the Government to protect the people, its corporate employees and consumers? But
how far? This is the battle ground.

Regulation has a cost to everyone-Government and as well as Corporations.
This is where we have to draw the line to see if the marketplace, Adam Smith's invisible
hand will do its work of limiting high prices because of competition and assure quality and
safety, being better than its competitors. Will the market economy priced fairly based on it

demand and supply? Equilibrium they say in economic terms, but it is not the market that

dictates prices it is the behavior of people in the market and I must say that behavior of people

is mostly irrational as opposed to rational. It was always taken for granted that people make

choices on rational behavior because they know what it are good for them. Not true.

Consumers don't think so because they are consumer magazines, consumer advocates,

consumer's associations, consumer's watchdogs and Government agencies checking what

could be toxic, dangerous and accidentally prone artifices for consumers.

Companies will say that they are too many laws, to many codes to obey, too many by-laws to

follow, labour laws to respect, too many government agencies to comply too but even at that

level of legislation and scrutiny, we find products and chemicals and drugs that are

detrimental to human use and consumption.

There is a new trend established by an Economics professor in Bangladesh where he sees an

opportunity for a corporation to become more social, behaving more like a citizen, more

responsible to people and its environment. Corporative people hate the word ''social'' and

immediately jump on their high and mighty horse because it sound like ''socialism'' contrary to capitalism. They remind us that profits are the name of the game, not benevolence.

Developing a moral responsibility is not changing the system, being a good citizen is not
eschewing the system. Not polluting the air and the rivers is not being ''socialist'' is it?

People want more out of corporations since they have accumulated power and more rights
than individuals made in recent years, thus creating an imbalance on the power scale. They want
Corporations to give back, more than sponsoring a junior baseball team. They want the
Corporation to care about their community.

Why companies should be philanthropists you might ask?

Because they have taken more from the world than individuals have.
Joe Bakan in his book,'' The Corporation-the pathological pursuit of profit and power''
interviewed Milton Friedman, the Chicago economist, the indisputable free enterprise
advocate, about the cost to society of having corporations polluting, taking space, and natural
resources, utilization of large trucks on the road, noise-pollution, etc. He bluntly said;
'' These are externalities.'' and doesn't go any further in his statement. In my book,
''externalities'' are *external cost* and there are *no external benefits*. This is where the work of
economists begin, evaluating the external cost to its surroundings, it's people, its environment in

the short and particularly long term; -anything outside the firm. Internal costs are done by
accountants, M.B.A's and engineers. Economics is a social behavioral science after all.

No wonder that J.M. Keynes came back in the limelight recently since he was the one
advocating governmental interference in a market economy. The social corporation can be constituted internally without interfering with its mission or
pro-profit endeavour. First, I would encourage every employee to become shareholders so
that they feel on the same level as management and participating in decision making. A payroll
deduction for the purchase of share is being already done and proved to be excellent for
morale and productivity. Instead of just an ordinary idea box, regular meetings should be
organized to solve production problems and political problems. Anything to bring closer the
cliff between employees and management.

Shareholders should have more say than just an annual vote. A visit to the plant, organizing an
information trip or weekend, to get closer to management and its operation. Wineries and
chocolate factories have a good sense of welcoming their clients, taking them for a tour,
testing products, telling them how it is done, being totally open.

I wouldn't suggest going around and tasting boiling chemicals, but you get the picture.

Even Volkswagen in Germany has an open plant, walls made out of glass as oppose to
concrete where employees can see outside and customers can see inside. One can walk
in and see their own vehicles being made on the spot and drive away with it. That is
transparency.

As oppose to have a board of directors full of entrepreneurs with a ''greed card'' hoping they
will get some stock real cheap and make a killing, it would be nice to have people from the
community that represents other people. I wouldn't go as far as inviting the local Chaplin and a
few Congregational nuns just to look good, but real people from serious organization that can
contribute positively with a different point of view and people with social responsibilities. It
could be a person from the employment office suggesting some kind of training program for
the younger generation and so forth.

There are many ways to give a ''heart'' to a company so that they see partners in
people as oppose of being strictly a labelled consumers.

People are tired to be viewed strictly as consumers where their opinion don't matter and their
''morale factor'' is being forgotten. The new movement is called the ''ethical consumer''
which encompasses more than quality and price, it is fair-trade, social accountability, organic
food, shade-grown coffee, free-range poultry, grass-fed beef, union–made, recycled,

sweatshop-free and environmentally friendly.

BIG PHARMA

Big pharmaceutical companies have been constantly criticized by many for their exaggerated prices they charge for their drugs, particularly when the drugs are a matter of life and death. Most cancer pills are extremely expensive so are HIV pills.

Most companies will justify the high cost by mentioning that the cost of research (R&D) is the main reason for the drug to be so expensive. It is difficult to argue about this particular point because we, the public don't really know, neither does the Government. The only thing I can say is that the demand for drugs to cure or reduce the effect of HIV and cancer is increasing every year. There is no shortage of ''clients'' with HIV (50% of Africans) and cancer patient increasing, should be making the mass fabrication of these drugs more affordable.

It is well known that Americans buy their drugs in Canada and Mexico and e-pharmacies because they can't afford the expensive price tags. When you are on a government pension, hundreds and thousands of dollars on medication puts elderly people in a financial bind.

Since most of these large corporations are public, we can certainly look at their profit margins if they are actually profiting from the helpless and the sick.

The first name which came to mind was **GlaxcoSmith Kline**, London based and U.S listed and I was lucky to find some latest news on their Avandia obligated to pull back.

''In September' European regulators ordered Avandia off the market and the U.S Food and Drug Administration restricted its use in the United States because of evidence that the drug

increased the risk of heart attacks. ''GlaxcoSK to take a $ 3.4 billion charge on Avandia.'' The company said the charge is in addition to the $ 2.4 billion announced in July. The company said it has continued to receive new claims. ''We recognize that this is a significant charge, but we believe the approach we are taking to resolve long term-standing legal matters is in the company's best interest, '' said P.D. Villareal, senior vice president for global litigation.
We see by his statement that shareholders come first not the victims which he calls, '' legal matters.''
''At this point, there no certainty that this charge will suffice the future claims, even if it seems a large amount.''
(Source: Yahoo Finance article, January 17, 2011).

Looking at the balance sheet, the $ 3.4 billion charge for future legal interference came at shareholders' expense when Operating Income came close to zero. EPS came at .02 cent in Q2 2010 but still the company bounce back the next quarter to .28 ESP. Sales and profit margin preserved.
Without being neither an accountant nor an analyst, this right off came at shareholders' expense and stock performance.
Being in the low 40's to a decline to $33.19 on July 11, 2009. Since then the stock has managed to go up again in his usual low 40's.
All the R&D expenses on Avandia didn't pay off and it's still $ 3.4 billion shy at shareholders' expense because sales and profit margin didn't bugged and neither total operating expense after the big boy's salaries and bonuses.
The company paid a $700 million in fines due to negligence and mix up of drugs fabrication.

Eli Lilly is another well-known company with healthy regular sales and profit margin reflected in the stock which is relatively stable. Only in June 2009 when operating profits slip a little and profit margin as well below 25% when the market

reacted pushing the stock at $32.02. It recuperated since then when the margin was back in line.
Return on equity was 53.25% for 2009 and 46.14% for Q1 2010.
The PE is at 8.0
Is this high return on equity exaggerated or simply expected?

Abbot Laboratories swings more in price on the market and operating profits and EPS. The PE is almost double Eli Lilly of 15 for some reason. Net income and profit margin have been going steadily down reflected in the stock price in mid-40 from a high of $56.79.
Like major international companies, licensing of new products and law suits from competitors affect perception of potential earnings, thus making the stock volatile.

Bayer AG is a holding company managing different smaller companies in different endeavours. It might be more difficult to analyze the Bayer group but the operating margin is much lower than competitors. The operating margin was 6.48% for Q3, 2010 and a net operating margin of 3.32% and return on assets of 2.24% and return on average equity of 6.02%
The price volatility is high on the market with a high PE of 27.6
Bayer is in a court battle for reverse payments, meaning paying off a company for delaying generic products. Legal battles of big pharmaceutical companies are intricate, to say the least, giving corporate litigators work for decades to come. Makes me wish I should have been a lawyer. (Again)

Bristol-Myer Squibb's finances seem to be right on the button with a net profit margin at 27% for Q3 and 23.5% for 2009. Operating margins are at 33.6% for Q3 and 29.79% for 2009. Return on average assets was 16.6 % for Q3 and 14.6% for 2009 and return on equity is 23.9% and 23.79% for their respective Q3 in 2009. PE is 13.3. Market price ranged in the last 52 weeks from $22 to $28, now $25.81.

Pfizer seems to be experiencing some difficulties in Q4 2010 versus 2009. Net profit margin went from 17.2% to 5.4% and operating margin of 21.65% to 8.9% and return on average assets were 5.33% now for Q4 is 1.8% and return on average equity is 4.0% from 11.69%.
Price range on the market is between $ 14.00 to $20 and now trading at $ 18.40 with a PE of 24.17.
In 2006/07 the stock was trading higher than $ 26 and fell gradually to today's price. There is nothing like a little trouble at the top to worry investors. R & D expenses were going nowhere when the CEO decided to scrap the project to find Lipitor's successor when a patient die in clinical trials.
Investors were not happy with the new CEO and the board as well since the stock was depressed since his appointment.
A clinical trial went wrong.
According to a recent article published by Dr. Mercola, Pfizer paid a fine of $75 million in a settlement with the Nigerian government for a clinical trial which killed 11 children with the drug Trovan.
I thought that pharmaceutical companies were there to cure health problems but we see that ''trails and error'' approach is a matter of money, not saving lives or cure diseases.

What I'm looking for is the excessive mark up on certain crucial drugs which I'm sure I won't find in the financial reports. Most international pharmaceutical companies operate under numerous private subsidiaries in various countries where certain clinical trials are more feasible and where the information is dispensed on a voluntary basis.
With 30 postings on the Income & Expense report, I'm sure there is plenty of room to hide excessive profits. I shall

concentrate on errors, lawsuits, government interventions and approvals.

In a recent article published by Dr. Mercola (e-mail letter) he quotes an article published in TIME magazine January 7- 2011 based on another article from the Institute of Safe Medication and Practices, which mentioned that some 31 drugs used for antidepressant are not working, not getting the effect desire since most patients still feel depressed and violent.

The top ten drugs were:

Varennicline (Chantix)-Fluoextine (Prozac)-Paroxetine (Paxil)-Amphetamines (various)-Mefoquine (lariam)-Automoextine (Strattera)-Triazolam (Halcion) Fluvoxamine (Luvox)-

Venlafaxine (Effexor) -Desvenlafaxine (Pristiq).

The increase of the use of antidepressant is staggering since there are so many now available and people are coming forward admitting openly their disease.

It seems like creating 31 different drugs for the same thing is more a trial and error strategy.

I cannot argue scientifically the pros and cons of each pill but I can certainly argue with the mathematics of it easily. It is simply impossible to introduce so many chemicals and know the reaction or the side effects they might cause. It is in the millions. So trial and error are still taking a big chance with peoples' lives and for what? Mass profits.

Even the ACS has been criticized, (American Cancer Society) for its absence to mention in Congress or out in the open what would be the cause of cancer. This lack of voice is blamed on the close ties the ACS has with companies that promote cancer pills and other medical equipment companies which are contributors to the Society.

In a long 130 page report from Dr. Samuel Epstein, chairman of the Cancer Prevention Coalition ''plainly lay's to bare the many conflicts of interest that hampers the effectiveness of this organization.''

His qualm is that many companies which support the ACS are in the chemical field, from pesticide to petrochemicals, cosmetic and the junk food industry, which are in fact contributors to cancer.

The other uneasiness Dr. Epstein has is the promotion of mammography to women twice a year as oppose to only once a year since it produces radiation and also not to mention that thermographic breast screening is far better than mammography which uses mechanical pressure or ionizing radiation-the two factors that can contribute to the creation of breast cancer.

Breast cancer is not something I've paid good attention too albeit that my sister had breast cancer six or seven years ago and that also men can have breast cancer. I concentrate my investigations more on prostate cancer and colon cancer. This to say that I personally don't hear much about preventive measures from the ACS and of being in the forefront of advocating changes in products and environmental conditions. We hear of the ''Walk Against Cancer'' but I wonder if this raising funds opportunity goes in the direction of its mission? I'm also skeptical about big charity organizations wondering how much of the donations go directly to people that needs it or the majority of the funds are used to keep the organization alive (administration) and keeping some executives away from the poor house and given the temptation to transfer some funds into their own bank account. I'm just saying.

After seeing the building where ACS resides on TV, I see a lot of money there. It is an architectural masterpiece. Makes you wonder if the money donated for medical research is being used for that purpose.

DR.BURZYNSKI'S CASE.

Speaking of big institutions and the way money flow to them and doesn't go where it should, the Dr. Burzynski's case with the FDA in the 80's right through 1995 is a good example. I didn't remember this unfortunate case of the 80's until today when Dr. Mercola's letter came on my computer. The letter summarizes the case based on the ''Video'' which is quite lengthy and revealing. I certainly won't try to summarize it because it won't do it justice but you can certainly watch it yourself. It is touching and quite revealing about the question of big institutions which are funded by large pharmaceutical companies for approval of their drugs.

Without trying to weight the two sides of the question, the FDA and Dr. Burzynski new drug at the time, ANTINEOPLASTON, I was convinced at the very beginning by the statements of cancer patients who were told that they had only a few months to live and only CHEMO and RADIATION would prolong their lives with detrimental side effects. The drug was efficient with excellent results but Dr. Burzynski couldn't get approval by the FDA and more so, the FDA tried for years to revoke his license as a doctor.

My experience with CHEMO and RADIATION extends to my wife's cancer in 1998 when she was faced with a recommendation of these conventional medical therapies.

We did look at other non-conventional remedies when we were told that that the possibility of complete curing even with chemo and radiation were slim. We didn't find out about Dr. Burzynski unfortunately but what we found was that there was a choice of only two types of chemicals in chemo and if that didn't work, **so be it.**

I was shocked to find out that the possible cures were so limited by conventional medicine.

There are actually four chemicals but they did narrowing it down to two.

<u>After 100 years of research and money is not an object if we
look at the ACS's books, how come they have come up with
only a hand full of destructive chemicals to cure cancer?</u>

The side effects were mentioned and they were many but
seemed worthwhile at the time.
I don't want to tell my story or my wife's because it is Dr.
Burzynski's story that I want to mention and for you to watch
for yourself. Please see; Dr. Mercola's site, library of videos.
I just want to mention that I was easily convinced by this
movie and emotionally disturbed after my experience with my
late wife.
My conclusion and *please reach your own*, that big institutions
and big pharmaceutical companies delve in billions of dollars
and this is where the partition is set. Money is the game and
certainly not the cure. Dr. Bursinski's Antinenoplaston would
have wiped out any other chemicals out there to cure cancer.
How come they haven't come up with a cure for the common
cold since they are hundreds of pill to *reduce or alleviate the
symptoms* but **not** actually cure it? This is pristine clear that
the pills or drugs are where the money lies, not the *actual
cure.*
July 29-2011
Abbott Laboratories is under a class suit for its popular drug,
''Biaxin,'' an antibiotic drug which has psychotic side effects.
A woman was found to cut her hand while making dinner
thinking it was a tomato. Twenty (20) other people joined the
lawsuit for having the psychotic effect or delusional behavior.
There is got to be a better way of producing drugs than on a
''trial and error'' approach.

OIL OR BLACK GOLD- TEXAS TEA.

We are certainly led to believe daily that we are at the mercy
of oil and there is a time factor
involve before we run out of it or the prices would be so high
that we are going to feel not
only at the mercy of oil companies but literally stranded on a
deserted road and left there to
rot for ever; out of gas.

In the short term, analysts say that oil prices will be going up
in the next two years to $150 a
barrel and on the other hand we are finding new places to
extract the precious liquid in North Dakota, Brazil, and
Alaska. We are looking in the Artic and pretty much all over
the world. The Athabasca Oil Sand in Alberta Canada is
valued to be the second largest reserve after Saudi Arabia and
a probability of being able to supply us for the next seventy
five years. Of course it is very expensive oil to extract but
there are coming out with new ways and cheaper ways to
extract the precious oil. There are the Colorado Oil Shells as
well waiting in the offing as a possible reserve and the rest of
the world. From Russia to Africa to Indonesia, the Middle
East, South and North America, oil is exploited out to supply
our capricious need.

Is this really something we are really going to run out off?

Using Malthusian thinking, population growth is inevitable
and is the base of concern to ask
yourselves if we are going to run out of petrol and food as
well. Technology did save us
increasing yields of crops and be able to feed the world but is
technology going to save us

again for our energy needs. Even looking for and producing energy, we need energy to do so.

We need natural gas to extract oil, we need electricity to operate machinery and we need
gasoline to transport oil and gasoline, we need coal to produce electricity. The more we look
and produce, the more we consume energy. Seems like a vicious circle, but energy is at the
base of practically everything.

Oil producers and suppliers.

Let's begin with the broad picture and refine (no pun intended) our way to the gas pump.
In North America we have; (2010)
Canada produces over 3 million barrels a day. (B/day)
United States produces over 9.5 million b/day.
Mexico produces 3 million b/day
Total in North America produces 15.5 million b/day

Argentina produces 795 th. B/day
Aruba produces 477th. B/day
Barbados in thousands
Belize in thousands
Brazil produces 2,700 million b/day
Chile in thousands
Colombia in thousands
Costa Rica is negative
Cuba in thousands
Dominican Republic is negative
Ecuador is half a million b/day

El Salvador is negative

Guatemala in thousands

Jamaica is negative as well as Martinique and Nicaragua and Paraguay

Peru in thousands

Netherlands Antilles minimum

Puerto Rico and Suriname and Trinidad & Tobago are minimum producers

Venezuela produces 2.350 million b/day

Total in Central and South America produces 7.5 million b/day

There are 30 countries in Europe producing 5 million b/day in total

leading by Norway for 2 million b/day

and United Kingdom (offshore) for 1.4 million b/day

Total in Europe for 5 million b/day

Total Eurasia (12 countries) including Russia produces 13 million b/day

Russia accounts for 10 million b/day.

The Middle East countries produce about 25 million b/day which includes;

Iran, 4.2 million

Iraq, 2.4 million

Kuwait, 2.5 million

Oman, 861 th. B/day

Qatar, 1.4 million b/day

Saudi Arabia, 10 million b/day

United Arab Emirates, 2,8 million b/day

Yemen, 264 th. B/day

In the African countries accounts for over 10 million b/day
divided in 20 countries leading by Algeria, 2.4 million b/day.

Asia and Oceania divided by 25 countries produces a total **of 8.5 million** leading by China with 4.2 million b/day.
In the world, all these countries produced around 85 million barrels a day in a given year.
Source: International Energy Statistics-EIA-U. S. Information Administration. 2010
Total Oil supply in millions Barrels per day.   (MBL/Day)

It is interesting to see who the big players are. The net exporters and who are the contributors or try to be self-sustained in the energy sector. They are more countries doing exploration but without any commercial findings.

THE USERS in numbers

All countries use oil and some more than others. Most would like to be self-sufficient but most import crude oil even Canada which also is an exporter of oil. It's only a question of transportation logistics but nevertheless it is frustrating to see an exporting country paying international prices for oil when we have plenty in our backyard. There is no relief nor discount and no price control for Canadian gas.
The United States consumes the most, well over the production amount. Like we saw earlier, it produces about 9.5 BL/day a day when its needs are 20 million BL/day. A shortage of roughly 10 million bbl./day or double the amount of what they produce. In percentage, the US consumes 24% of the world oil produced while its population represents 3% of the world.
The European Union consumes 14.4
China 8.0
Japan 4.7
Russia 2.8
India 2.7
Brazil 2.5

Saudi Arabia 2.4
Canada 2.2
South Korea   2.1
Mexico 2.1
Iran 1.7
Indonesia 1.5
There are 11 countries which consume less than 1,000,000 BL/Day and 30 countries with
less 500,000 BL/Day out of 208 countries reported in World Factbook (2008) listed on Wikipedia.
The exact number is not important because it changes all the time and by the time one computes the numbers they have already changed. It is *the relativity* that counts and who is oil rich and oil poor and who is relatively dependant or in a dire straight for oil.

To recap by continents, North America consumes 24.3 b/day and produces 16.0 b/day
Europe Union consumes 15.5 and produces 5.0 b/day
China produces half its need as well by consuming 8.0 and producing 4.2 b/day
Russia consumes 2.8 b/day and produces 13 b/day
India consumes 2.7 and produces 880,000 b/day
Saudi Arabia consumes 2.4 and produces 10.0 b/day
Brazil consumes 2.7 and produces 2.4 b/day
There is no point of listing all the 208 countries of what they produces and consumes but in general it is mentioned that we produce 85.0 bbl./day *worldwide* and consumes 85.9 bbl./day.
Conclusion: I would consider this a tight market, or equilibrium, using an economic expression.
Are we more knowledgeable now than we started with?
We knew this at the start that the US was starving for oil but we want to know about the future and the volatility of the gasoline prices at the pump. It is good to know the "have and the have not" in the oil import and export first. The world

market aspect of this commodity is more complex has we shall see. We are also interested in China since it is the fastest growing country in economic growth and of population growth and India as well.

European countries consume three times as much as being produce and the US and China and India consumes twice as much as being produces. That is the story in a nutshell.

So far we have identified the players and in which corner they sit.

Wherever there is a car, it needs gasoline, whatever small the territory.

Yes, the full battery cars are underway.

OIL MARKETS

Since crude oil is coming from different corners of the world and going all over the world, there are many listed markets:
-West Texas Intermediate
-North Sea Brent
-Persian Heavy
-Bonny Light
-Ural/Mediterranean
-And OPEC Daily basket.
Like oil, from crude to refine, there are different allocations.
Distillate Fuel Oil
Jet fuel
Motor gasoline
Residual fuel oil (used for asphalt-lubricant etc.)
SPR fuel (reserve)
To reiterate our primary interest is to see if gasoline prices reflect the imports shortage (or supply) if any. Let's get down to brass tack.

Motor Gasoline Retail, US. City Average (cents per gallon, including taxes)

For all types of gasoline, we have monthly averages beginning in 2008 to 2010.

In 2008:

January-the price went from 309.6 cents to close with an average of 331.7 cents.

But in July it was 411.5 and August 414.2 the vacation months.

It was below average in December at 174.2 and January 2009 at 183.8

In 2009:

January prices were 183.8 as mentioned,

and July and August they were 259.4 and 267.7 respectively with an yearly average of 240.1

In December prices were 267.1.

In 2010:

January prices were 277.9 and an annual average of, NA.

July and August prices were 278.3 for both months but October they were 284.3

The prices in December were not compiled yet but in my city of Montreal, the prices went up at least 10% in mid-December. These figures show that there is a Christmas price and a holiday price as well, substantially above the yearly average.

Refiner Prices of Petroleum to End Users (cents per gallon, excluding taxes)

Years 2008 were:

January 257.1

June was 358.0

July were 356.8

December were 121.9 with an average of 277.5

Years 2009 were:

January 135.8

June was 218.7

July were 206.7

December were 214.4 with an average of 188.8

Year 2010 was:

January was 224.0

June was 225.1

July were 224.7   note that April and May were 237.0 235.3 respectively.

It seems that the summer pattern is still in force but not for Christmas. In 2008 and 2009,

the winter holidays there was a relief, off the average.

For the summer holidays we can estimate that refiners control the getaway

fuel and retailers are passing it on.

It's worth noticing that refiners prices took off in 2007 at 234.5 an average based on 2006 of 212.8 and from 182.9 in 2005. Refiner's margins are also different from the East coast to the West coast, Gulf coast and Mid-Continent due to transportation which is a major contributor of the cost, using gasoline as well.

Petroleum trade: Export/ Imports (Millions Barrels per day) in North America.

Since 1996, total imports have not changed much, from 9,478 to 13,468 in 2007. It equals up to 30% increase in approximately ten years. In the year 2008 total oil imports were relatively the same at 12,915. It was less in 2009 at 11,691 and 2010, total oil imports were 11,849.

The average in 2008-09 didn't change much from the years 2000.

There is no significant increase in Imports for the months of June and July and December for crude oil for the years under observation; 2008-2009-2010.

There are no significant increases in Exports from the US to other countries around 2,000 since the summer of 2008. As I mentioned before in regards to North America, the US and Canada, both country's imports and export crude oil in order to minimize transportation cost. There are trade zones which are more efficient rather than transporting from coast to coast. The West trades with the West and the Great Lakes Region together and East Canada with New England.

US imports from OPEC countries didn't change much either since 1998, around 5,000 and a slight increase in 2008 to an average of 5,954 and a decrease in 2009 to 4,776 and back to 5,013 in the year 2010.

The monthly imports were the same as the yearly average for July, August, and December.

In other words, it is not OPEC that wants to make sure we spend more at Christmas and in the summer holidays to choke our economy. (Just in case you wondered) They surely want us to prosper and buy more cars.

The percentage of imports from OPEC and the Persian Gulf didn't change either. From 40% from OPEC and 17.0% from the Gulf in 2005 to 40.9 % and 14.6% on the average in 2009, with a slight increase in 2008. US Import from non-OPEC countries even declined from 8,190 in 2006 to 7,139 in 2009 and 6,968 in 2008.

Petroleum Stock (billion barrels) has steadily increased from 1,000 in 1973 to 1,665 in 2007 and 1737 in 2008 and 1776 in 2009 and to 1865 in last September of 2010.

Source: U.S. Energy Information Administration/Monthly Energy Review November 2010.

My conclusion of my bird's eye view of supply and demand and prices is that we are paying more for *storage* of oil as opposed to pay more for a shortage of exploration, production, or shipment of refiner's capacity or retailer's boldness or substantial increase in consumer demand.

Like any market, the exchange is done in anticipation of future prices rather than actual supply and demand. It is the psychological reflections of the markets which is more the anticipating of increase in demand that boost gas prices to go up. It is the same as anticipated profits of a company on any exchange. The price goes up before the Financials are released.

We will look at the profits of major public oil and gas companies to prove my point.

One thing thought is that we are not running out of oil, we are running out of cheap oil.

Since exploration cost is escalating, we can no longer find it in our backyard.

PROFITS FOR US MAJOR OIL PRODUCERS (in USD)

	2009-	2008-	2007-	2006-	2005
EXXON MOBIL-($74.90) Year					
Gross Operating Profits:	52,891	94,542	84,795	82,628	73,657
EPS:	3.99	8.78	7.36	6.68	5.76
TOTAL S.A ($54.89)	58,568	67,866	70,800	64,721	59,469
EPS:	5.44	6.59	8.53	6.77	6.19
ROYAL DUTCH SHELL ($67.4)	52,610	74,329	70,553	66,909	66,090
EPS:	4.08	8.54	10.00	7.94	7.58
BP Oil S.A.($46.36)	47,430	57,570	52,915	50,164	52,164
EPS:	5.31	6.67	6.53	6.69	10.76
CVX($91.05)	30,959	50,294	40,261	39,870	31,957
EPS:	5.26	11.74	8.83	7.84	6.58
CONOCO PHILLIPS ($67.39)	20,376	39,724	34,335	35,317	26,938
EPS:	3.26	-11.16	7.32	9.80	9.79

Source: Bloomberg Financial

The year 2008 was an outstanding year for most of them gross profit wise and earnings per share.

Except for Conoco Phillips which had some substantial write offs and Total S.A. with a small decrease in gross profits and EPS.

If we look back on our data, we see that motor gasoline prices increased in 2008 as well as refiner's prices. They're a steady average of imports of 12,915 MB/day and a small increase mostly from OPEC but a decrease in imports from non-OPEC producers. Petroleum stock has had a steady increase since 1973 right up to 2010. The price of crude oil on the international market hit a high in July 2008 up to $147.00 a barrel.

Without being a forensic accountant, we can see that the market and the supply were relatively steady in 2008 except the retail prices of gasoline and refinery prices and crude oil. In conjuncture with increase in profits from these six major oil companies (except one), and the increase in stock of oil, I can honestly say that we've paid for hording or stocking crude oil at bigger profits, thus at cheaper cost for the companies. Stocking crude oil is not a bad thing *per se* but it triggers the question why at this particular point in time. I think we should look at world events to see if there were not tragedies that influenced the apprehensiveness of future oil shortage since markets react on chaos and fear and anticipation.

I'm sure that my theory is oversimplified because they are more players in the oil market like speculators which drives the price upward. The futures market attracts big players like banks and other large financial institutions. But like any other market, it is a psychological game as much as the currency market and the stock market. Some thrive on bad news because it is time to make serious money and it is more predictable. Shorting banks stock and mortgage company's stock made billions for some investors in 2008-2009 or should I say; ''for dis-investors.''

The rise of ''disaster capitalist'' has been around for quite a while because it is easier to predict the reactions of people and

Governments when they are vulnerable and have limited choices.

As far as the argument goes that we should at least invest in oil companies to recoup our losses at the pump, holders of these six major oil companies were rewarded from 2007 to half of 2008 until they all followed the decline of the Dow Jones Index and the S&P 500 after the financial breakdown. During the year of 2008 was the most profitable year and if you were long on their stock and didn't sell on time, you experience quite a loss. So much for fundamentals.

Market reactions and good earnings are not compatible as one is lead to believe. That is why I call the stock market (all other markets as well) a psychological indicator. Stock prices don't represent intrinsic value and the currency itself doesn't have real value. It is part of our belief or and exchange system. I'm sure there must be a few accountants saying, '' what?'' Sorry but this is what I believe.

In 2008, when we slide in into a major recession, oil companies were having their best year in earnings. The market hit an all-time high and the stock of oil increased as well, not the imports, like we are lead to believe, that OPEC is toying with us. We've paid extra for *hording* crude oil because we were in a financial crisis when the real estate market crashed followed by a credit crunch. Again, the oil companies came out smelling like roses until the following year, 2009, when we were in the heart of the recession and price fell.

They played on our uncertainties and our fears in this financial collapse.

Again, they have given us the finger .

THE FUTURE'S MARKET
The futures market is quite large since it does involve many commodities and many players.

It was created to protect or freeze prices of an underlying commodity at a future date. It does protect producers and also big users to be able to confirm prices for a later date.
Not all participants are producers and users. Anybody can buy contracts for speculation and re-sale before the limit date.
There are options (puts & calls) and one can sell short as well. They say that speculators provide liquidity to the market beside the real users and producers.
Who are the speculators?
First; the EIA org. names those, commercial participants (those that have a direct in the physical (let say oil) production, consumption, or trade.) The non-commercial investors (money managers and funds and banks and brokers) are interested of trading contracts for investment and diversification. All are done on the exchange of the NYMEX.

The EIA published a graph on the open interest of oil future from the year 2000 to this day.

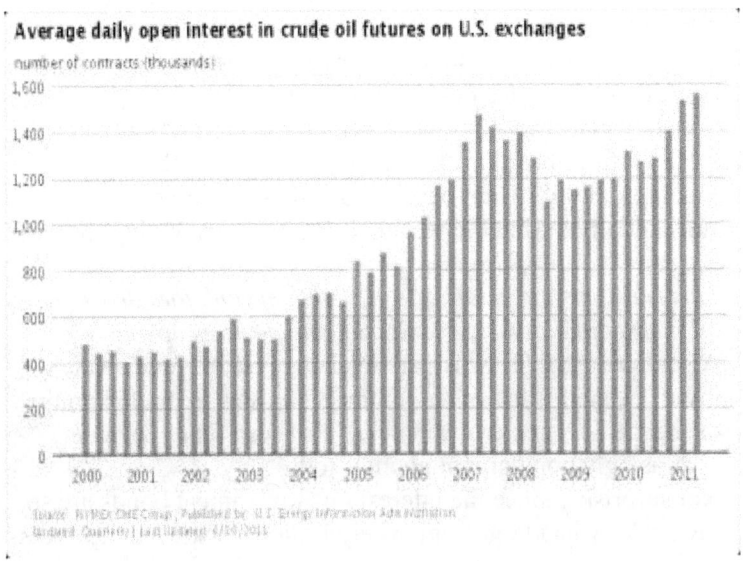

Average daily open interest in crude oil futures on U.S. exchanges

Since 2004 right through its peak in 2007, open interest has been climbing rapidly to decrease slowly in 2009 during the recession year and then back up in 2010 and 2011.

The EIA itself mentioned that; ''non-commercial commodity trading and investment may use up liquidity and amplify price movements, particularly when momentum is running strongly in a particular direction.''

The open interest can be checked on the New York Mercantile Exchange (NYMEX).

There is also the OTC, over the counter exchanges where the big players are ready to exchange between themselves some major blocs. The OTC is a pre-market trading before the NYMEX opens for all traders. The EIA mentioned that it is difficult to know who trades the most since it is not evident who trades on the OTC. So much for transparency.

''On a net basis (subtracting short positions from long positions), physical participants tend to be net *short* while traders in the money managers category tend to be net *long*.'' EIA org.

In other words, there is more money chasing the contracts that there should be, thus pushing up prices.

''Money managers have been net long in their U.S exchange-traded futures positions for the vast majority of the time since January of 2008. Their net long position increased substantially during the recent period of unrest in the Middle East and North Africa.''

This is as pristine clear as it gets, that speculators drove the oil market and other agricultural commodities upwards.

Also there are ETF which are exchange traded funds which invest in energy and other commodities and are traded on the exchange like stocks. The interest on those funds became increasingly popular among investors.

Not surprising since the interest on Government bonds are so low, money had to go somewhere beside stocks. All the excess

money of QE2 did not go to the proper hands, the small and mid-size business in order to be able to create jobs.
It went in the financial markets like stocks, commodities.
Even the EIA organization admits that the situation is ''kind of fuzzy'' to try to pinpoint
which factors contributed the most of the price increases in commodities since there are other factors involved.'' Prices of crude oil and other commodities started to move together in recent years.''

Commodity Index assets under management and Dow Jones Index level

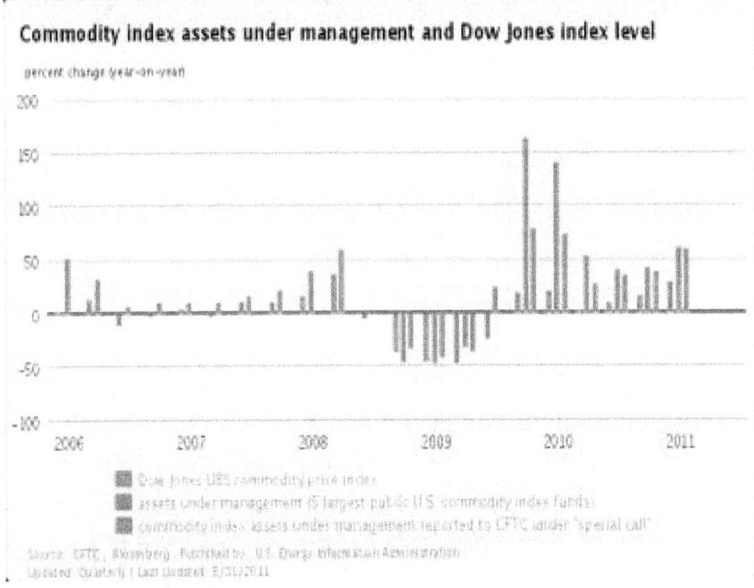

''Commodity Index investment flows have tended to move together with commodity prices.''

U.S. exchange-traded futures positions by money managers

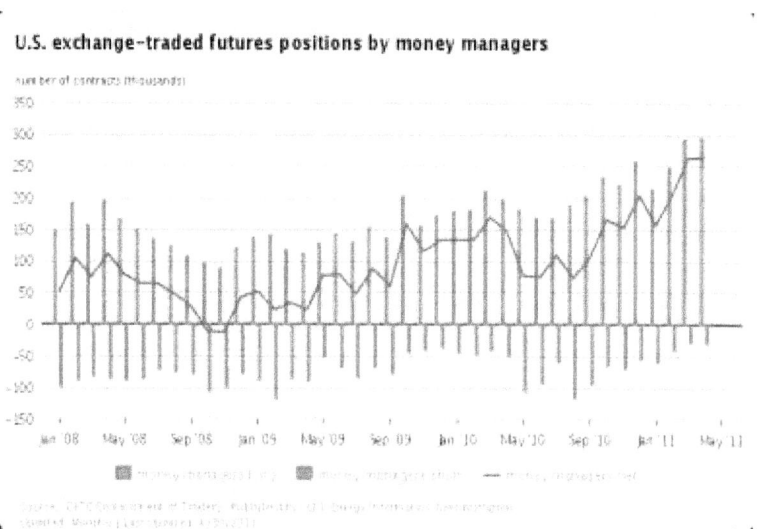

U.S. exchange-traded futures positions by producers, merchants, processors, and end users

42

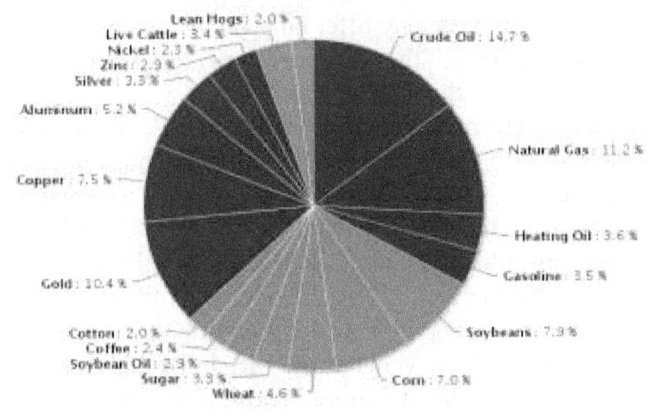

Composition of the Dow Jones UBS commodity index

2011 Target Weights of the Dow Jones – UBS Commodity Index

Lean Hogs: 2.0 %
Live Cattle: 3.4 %
Nickel: 2.3 %
Zinc: 2.9 %
Silver: 3.3 %
Aluminum: 5.2 %
Copper: 7.5 %
Gold: 10.4 %
Cotton: 2.0 %
Coffee: 2.4 %
Soybean Oil: 2.9 %
Sugar: 3.3 %
Wheat: 4.6 %
Corn: 7.0 %
Soybeans: 7.3 %
Gasoline: 3.5 %
Heating Oil: 3.6 %
Natural Gas: 11.2 %
Crude Oil: 14.7 %

Source: Dow Jones Indexes, CME Group. Published by: U.S. Energy Information Administration
Updated: Annually | Last Updated: 2011

I couldn't say it better myself, *that speculation* is at the base of rising prices.

After all these proofs when reading the material, the EIA comes with this statement;
'' Some market observers believe that the increased trading activity by investors and long-only index finds in oil markets has had a significant impact on the energy price formation process. Although a growing body of research by academics and securities market analyst examines the issue, no definitive conclusion either proving or disproving a causal linkage between non-commercial trading and large energy price swings over the past few years has been reached.
Additional data and analysis are needed to better understand the relationship between energy derivative and price movements. In addition, the global nature of trade energy-related derivatives adds to the challenges of analyzing trading

activity. Because the vast majority of positions are held in the less transparent OTC derivatives market, however, analysis that relies only on the readily available data from the transparent portion may offer only limited insights.''
It is easy to see that the OTC investors are pulling the wool over the eyes of this institution.
The CFTC (Commodities Future Trading Commission) admitted openly that there were falling behind and had neglected some surveillance lacking of delegated powers to be able to scrutinize investors in the commodities market.
This is proof in the pudding. But wait, there is more.
''The CFTC mentioned that the price of crude oil showed *positive correlation* with stocks from 2008-2010, and *negative correlation* with the value of the U.S dollar during most of late 2007 to the present, and more irregular but *negative correlation* with the bond prices during 2008-2010.''
In other words, positive correlation means going in tandem with and negative correlation means going to the contrary. Commodities prices and the stock market moved in the same directions since the bond market didn't offer positive yields and the currency was devaluating itself daily against other currencies. Where to go but stocks and commodities?
I don't think it is positive economic expectations since the recovery didn't show signs of a takeoff. For a speculator ''working the news'' and trading on a daily basis, economic expectations are not part of his strategy. Since there his puts and calls and selling short, only movement is needed on a daily basis. Only a few percentages a day makes quite a bundle at the end of the month. One has the possibility of doubling his money every month, if he is not wrong too many times.
As foreign oil (Brent) goes upward, does have a double effect on consumers. Since the Trade Balance of the US increases it is also putting downward pressure on the dollar, thus lessening the purchasing power of American consumers.

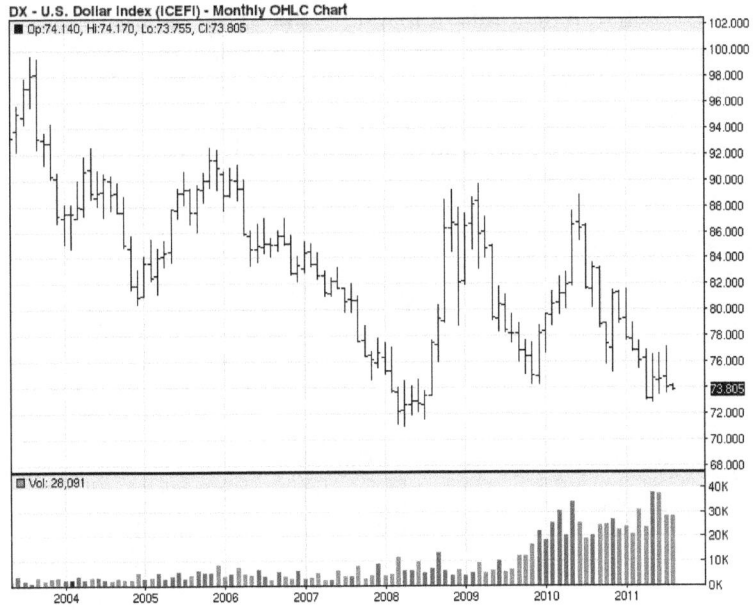

DX - U.S. Dollar Index (ICEFI) - Monthly OHLC Chart
Op:74.140, Hi:74.170, Lo:73.755, Cl:73.805

Should we worry about the Future's market of commodities compared with the spot market?

These two markets are parallel to each other but not the same. The spot market is between farmers and distributors with some marketing agencies in between like AMS and FAO and the SMS to help inform farmers and traders on the current price and availability. The farmers can also keep abreast of prices through MIS, the Market Information Services.

Wholesale prices are also available for farmers from kiosks and cafes to obtain information.

This has nothing to do with the futures' market. The future's market has been established to protect future positions for producers and large distributors. It is the financial aspect of commodities but not the real demand and supply pricing. The Futures' market like the stock market is the expectations of prices in the future. What people think, not the reality. The only reality in the future's market is that it has to be a representation of actual prices given a margin between real and possible prices.

CHAPTER TWO-

World news affecting oil markets

On the latest news (FEBRUARY FIRST 2011) (CNN News) there is turmoil in Egypt since a week, in Cairo to be precise where people are demonstrating after Jordan and Tunisia, where people are fed up of their present governmental ruling. *The price of oil just hit over $100.00 (Brent oil market) because of the turmoil in those countries, are reporting the experts. It is an all- time high since 2008.*
Funny enough that on my producer's list, Egypt is not there, at least doesn't produce significant amount, neither is Jordan and Tunisia. It is worth to re-check those figures again to see if the worrisome reaction is warranted or just a market heist, again.

Looking at the 2008 report from the CIA World Factbook, Egypt produced 630,000 B/day, being ranked 28 on the world's producer -Tunisia produced 52,000 B/day being 86th in the world producers and Jordan produced nothing. This is why I didn't mention it on a world scale since they *are insignificant players* .
Again, this is banking on turmoil in the political arena, not the supply of crude oil.
There is a war in Iraq, (seven years now) being a major player in the oil market, but did it affect the oil supply? The Americans made sure *not to affect* supply. What can be worse as far as drama to a country than fighting a war?

CL - Crude Oil WTI (NYMEX) - Monthly OHLC Chart
Op:96.20, Hi:96.60, Lo:92.77, Cl:93.50
Vol: 623,112

FEBUARY 3 -2011 (CNN News)
The news from Cairo is getting much worse. Since the announcement from Mubarak, (that he won't run again) the people have formed two distinct groups, the pro Mubarak and the ones who still want him out of office right away. The clash has created some lives lost (6) and hundreds of injuries. Gunshots were fired from the army, escalating the situation in general. Oil prices rose to $102.17 (Spot Brent)
(Source: Bloomberg daily report)
and natural gas to 7.42($MMBTU) a 30% increase. Natural gas was lagging behind oil prices, meaning the spread in energy equivalent was the widest.
One factor we have to watch is the Suez Canal activity, if it is going to experience some turmoil and affect the shipment of crude oil. It is worth mentioning that the canal belongs to the Egyptian government since it nationalization in 1956 and there are no locks to operate it, like the Panama Canal does. There

are no restrictions as to who can go through. There was a single statement in the news this week, mentioning it might be a concern at this time. We shall follow the events.

FRIDAY -FEBUARY 4- 2011 (CNN News)

Tahir square is still busy with demonstrators now attacking the media people reporting on the situation. It is escalating judging by the number of deaths. Mubarak said he wants to step down but doesn't want his country creating chaos. I think chaos is seemingly present.

The price of the Brent Spot was down a shade to 101.62 $MMBTU but the US reserve rose 600,000 barrels to 38.8 million barrels, a record high. (Source: Bloomberg news.) One reporter said the region is jittery since Iraq oil shipment goes through Suez Canal even if Egypt is not a big player in the crude oil business. As I mentioned before, there are no locks to be operated and Egyptians seem to have their hands full with their riots.

The US is making pressure to tell Mubarak to step down immediately. I think the Canadian government will follow suit after deliberating the point for a few days. (??? !!!)

How much time one needs to figure out that you have to give what the people want. I think it is called democracy. Countries belong to its citizens and so does the governments as well. Governments don't own their countries; the people own governments and they are there only to rule for the people.

FEBRUARY FITH-2011 (CNN News)

A natural gas pipeline going to Jordan has been sabotaged in the near town of El Arish (on fire) in Egypt. Prices of commodities were negative (dated February fourth by Bloomberg). I don't think it is related to the present crisis but prices of oil and natural gas are not affected upwards. We will see today's prices posted tomorrow.

FEBRUARY SIX 2011 (CNN NEWS)

In the 13 days of the riot, the recent statements of changes seem to appease things on the street where people are behaving more docile in their demonstrations. Governmental changes did not actually happen yet and people want to see real changes and Mubarak actually stepping down.
There is no change in gasoline retail prices in the US since January 17, even a decline of .009 a gallon. (Source: EIA. doe. Gov.)
In Montreal, the newspapers stipulate that gas prices are the highest in Canada, 1.21238 $ liter, compared with Alberta of $ 1.0100 liter. (Source: gasbuddy. com)
Crude oil remained $91.00 in the US (Texas crude Intermediate) and gasoline prices stable.
Conclusion: The Egyptian crisis did not influence the international crude oil market much and not the US market. The gasoline market remained stable as well in the US and in Canada.
Our belief to begin with is; that they shouldn't be an increase in both crude oil and refine gas, since Egypt is not a major player in the oil business. So far we haven't been duped about a local crisis that influences international prices. More to follow.

FEBRUARY 8-2011 (CNN News) Cairo.

On the 15th day of the crisis, nothing is resolved even if Mubarak wants to amend the constitution.
The changes promised are not the removal of its president, who stubbornly hangs on to power.

On the economic side, having people not working, spending their time in the street, is contributing to a slowdown in productivity, creating a shorting on local goods.

One way that Egypt is affecting the world which is telling the other countries to face their governments and show how people should show their discontent towards present economic injustice.

People in Jordan are on the street utterly feed up of high food prices. Tunisia and Algeria as well, demonstrating about higher food prices. Food prices have not been as high since 2008 pretty much all over the world.

As Oil is concern today, the Brent crude future remains over 100 and the spread of the future's market and the WTI (West Texas Intermediate) ($ 86.90) is around $13.00 which is wider than it was a few days ago of $9.00.

Gold is up and silver and Wheat (KCB) and (CBT) as well by 1.70 and 1.86% respectively.

Gasoline futures (RBOB) are up 1.91%.

(Source: Bloomberg.com)

Should we worry about higher food prices all around the world?

Is it really that we are running demand side close to supply side?

Is it the Egyptian crisis that might increase the price of oil, the stopping of the canal Suez traffic which will affect the price of oil all over the world or the bad weather which affected crops in Australia and Brazil and the droughts in the US? Or all the above?

Food experts say that food prices will be going upward in 2011.

It means that supply is tight on all commodities and China is trying to reduce exporting inflation which is a factor on demand for food around the world. We can always blame China's growth for increasing demand for all things can we?

One thing for sure is that ''fear'' fulfills its own prophecy. ''The only thing we have to fear is fear itself.''- quote from Franklin D. Roosevelt.

I'm sure that food companies and individual around the world are stocking on non-perishable commodities just in case, thus creating higher present demand.

Again, that's what markets are all about, anticipating the future. The ''psychological index'' as they call it. I will watch the CPI (our own CPI) or Bloomberg's Commodities Price Index (on page 241) reported hourly as oppose the official CPI from the Bureau of Labour Statistics which is lagging behind and not as accurate and see if we can find out the real culprits of price increase of food; hype or reality?

FEBRUARY 9TH.2011 (CNN News)

There are no changes in the Egypt situation but they do mention a drought in China which will affect June crop of wheat. That will increase the importation of wheat by China but this excess demand be enough to raise international prices? Again, China is made the scapegoat of all rising prices.

Wheat Future (CBT) USD /bu. of 0.97% On Bloomberg commodities future it is worth to mention *the rise* of WHEAT (yesterday)

Wheat Future (KCB) UBD/bu. of 0.93%

And Coffee. C Future USD/lb. of 2.48%

On the same token, on CNN news, Carl Weinberg from High Frequency Economics was interviewed and asked if China was the major threat of world-wide inflation. ''China's inflation is 4.5% and annual growth of 9.75% which was predicted. Taken both these numbers, there is no real threat that this level of inflation will affect world inflation.''

FEBRUARY 11TH. 2011 (CNN News) -Cairo

According to Mubarak's speech yesterday, he made publicly
that he won't step down before new election time in
September. The crowd reacted negatively, putting more
pressure on the military which so far, have been on the side of
the people but this last avowal might trigger more violence on
the streets.
The Brent crude oil future climbed by 0 .90% to 101.78 and
the WTI Crude remained stable to $86.33, a spread of $15.54.
Some military force moved to Suez to protect the canal.
The latest news at 11.25 (EST) is that president *Mubarak is
stepping* down leaving the leadership of the country to a
council, announced the vice president. People are reacting
positively .

SATURDAY FEBRUARY 12-2011

The aftermath of Mubarak stepping down did influence the oil
price go down a bit.
Brent Crude Future was down 0.500% and the WTI crude
future was down 1.150% to $85.58.
Commodities in general were mixed but mostly down except
for Corn, up 1% and Cotton was up 1.7%. I can live with an
increase of Cotton. There were no substantial movements in
commodities. Source: Bloomberg.com (commodities, daily
prices)
For all intent and purposes, since the crisis in Egypt, the oil
price (WTI) did vary from mid- eighties to $91.66 and then
back today to $ 85.58 a barrel. We can round it off to a 7%
swing since the political turmoil. Since we mentioned that
Egypt was not a big player in the oil export business except
from the Suez Canal point of view, the one with no locks, was
the swing of international or national prices warranted?

Is 7% swing logical uncertainty, or a scare tactic to profit traders?
Was it hyped by the media or is it worthy of mention?

MONDAY FEBRUARY 14-2011

Egypt is politically turning the corner influencing other countries demonstrating their discontent about their leadership. There are some price hikes worth mentioning;
BRENT Crude Future USD/bbl. To $103.710 + 2.74%
WTI Crude Future USD/bbl. $85.87 + 0.34%
Gas Oil Future   + 2.38%
Gasoline RBOB Future USD/gal. + 3.17%
Wheat future (CBT)   USD/bu.   +1.31%
Wheat Future (KCB)   USD/bu.   +1.37%

In the countries now under observations: Algeria-Bahrain-Iran-Iraq-Jordan-Libya-Palestine Territories-Syria-Sudan-Tunisia-Yemen, where political unrest is present in the streets, some are exporters of oil as we mentioned (see page 20). In that respect, it would explain the Oil Future Index up to 103.71 (+2.74%) and the GAS Future by 3.17%. Again, the traders and speculators are jittery concerned by the possible shortage at this point. OPEC announced that the recession is over and they are not anticipating an increase of the price of oil. At this point, they don't want to see a substantial price increase since the demand have picked up and they don't want demand choking on high prices.
The latest Gas retail in the US by EIA.com is dated February 7-2011, with no increase in prices but we will see on the next compilation if there is any increase based on the Future Index. There is no news to explain the increase of Wheat futures besides that China is deemed to hoard the commodity. Again, China is to blame in the wheat increase in demand.
True or false?

FEBRUARY 15-2011 (CNN News)

While eleven countries mentioned above have joined the club
of protestors, Egypt is still in turmoil since more people are
demanding respective equality as far as salaries are concerned.
It seems that things are not back to normal.
In the commodity prices, only Coffee shows an increase of
1.34% to 265.200 USD/lb. and
Cotton 1.75% increase. (Source: Bloomberg.com-commodities
future index)

FEBRUARY 16-2011 (CNN News)

In the dozen countries experiencing political turmoil, nothing
has changed much besides some commodity prices have
moved: Sugar, 4.93%-Cocoa 1.69%-Coffee 0.88% Lean Hogs
1.57%.
It is to be noted that Corn increase is due to the use of making
Ethanol, an additive for motor gasoline. We commented on
that before that we are using food commodities for feeding
cars when food prices are going upwards!!! Quite a paradox!
Witnessing an interview with commodity trader Greg Smith
on Bloomberg.com, he says that prices of food commodities
will still go up and so will petrol which is an underlying cost
of all foods. His reason is; ''the growing demand for all foods
due to world growing population
and depleting food stock''. If this is the case, this is quite
serious. It is a Malthusian view where population increase will
surpass food production. We were saved once by the creation
of fertilizers which increased yields of crops, but have we
come to another realistic threshold?

ZW - Wheat (CBOT) - Monthly Line Chart
ZWU11: 684–4

FEBRUARY 17-2011 (CNN News) -Bahrain in the spotlight.

Egypt's domino effect has taken a turn rapidly from peaceful to violence in Bahrain. Three individuals were reported killed and the upset continues.

Bahrain is a major player in the oil business not by its low production of 40,000 b/d but in relevancy to its total revenues from oil products being ''the transporter'' for other countries like S.A who doesn't have access the Persian Gulf. Sixty percent of government revenues rely on oil base products and transportation (pipeline). The US does have some stake in this play since they own 40% of Caltex, a major oil company.

The Commodity Future Indexes are on the move:

Brent Crude Future to $103.72

WTI C. F. to $85.400

Coffee "C' F. 267.150 + 2.12%
Cotton no. 2 F. 201.93 + 3.59%
Soybean F. /bu. $ 1,405.00 +1.92%
Oat F. bu. $422.500 + 2.55%
Rough Rice (CBOT) $14.96 +1.98%
Soybean Meal F. 374.800 + 1.79%
Wool F (SFE) 1,173.00 +3.71%
(The rest had modest changes.)
(Source: Bloomberg news.com)
I'm mostly concerned about Oil and Food commodities which some experienced a substantial daily increase but I have yet to figure out why the rapid increase of Cotton and Wool.

FEBRUAY 18-CNN News

Libya seems to be taking the limelight on international unrest. Bahrain's center is quieting somewhat. Most commodities are down except for coffee and cocoa are still up.
Let's reiterate the reasons the newspaper reporters are giving for commodity price increases:
-Climate change- we have seen many floods and droughts over the past months.
-Speculation-some people speculate on the futures market and the spot market and hoarding physically some commodities.
-Food is being used for making ethanol, like corn and sugar cane and beets.
-The increase in demand worldwide caused by the increase of the population.

FEBRUARY 19-CNN News.

Coffee and Cocoa are still rising to 273.00 lbs. and $ 3,499 MT/USD.
Libya's unrest is rising.

KCU11 - Coffee (ICEUS) - Daily OHLC Chart
Op:240.60, Hi:243.70, Lo:240.10, Cl:241.35
Vol: 3,770

CCU11 - Cocoa (ICEUS) - Daily OHLC Chart
Op:2,974, Hi:2,984, Lo:2,950, Cl:2,950
Vol: 2,396

FEBRUARY 21-CNN News

Libya has turned into a war zone. 233 dead estimated so far.
The army-police and separatist groups are creating a civil war
premise. Gadhafi's son is trying to patch things up.
Libya being an oil rich country has its effect on oil prices.
Brent Crude Future to $104.21
and the WTI Crude Future to $88.85 and Silver F. is 33.36 up
3.29%.
The WTI Cushing Spot is at $86.20
So far, the supply side (production & inventories) is not
directly affected as yet.
The futures market is anticipating a rise due the crisis.
There might be an indirect effect on prices of oil since there it
is mentioned how China is ''coal hungry,'' the other fossil
fuel. It was stated before and accentuated again today.
Hype or reality?

FEBRUARY 22-2011-CNN News

Libya's situation is not improving and neither is Yemen.
Gadhafi's strong hold will simply enlighten the situation. Now
you have Morocco that has joined the revolution. We are
worried about oil & gas prices and commodities. Gas has been
up for two weeks ($3.17 gal.) but more data are underway.
One commodity is making a substantial rise is silver at $32.87
oz.
The headlines are scary, mentioning the possibility of $50.00
oz. for silver and $5,000. oz. for gold.
Libya produces less than 2 million barrels a day being the 18th
country in rank and Yemen around 300,000 Mbday, a small
producer.
Bloomberg commodities Index:

Brent crude F. $105.86
Heating Oil F. 279.040 + 2.86%
Gasoline RBOB   F.   261.180 + 2.37%
WTI is $91.20 Cushing from $86.00 +5.80%
US Retail gasoline is at $3.17 average, from $3.51 a month
ago but an increase from two weeks. These would have to
check with more recent data yet to be published.
There is no doubt that there is a crisis around the world in a
dozen countries plus the earthquake in New-Zealand affected
the international community and also affected international
prices of crude oil and gasoline and we are bracing for the
agricultural commodity price hikes.
But even though the situation is quite serious in the Middle
East and Iran is showing its fists as well, it is not still hype as
far as prices is concerned? *This is the premise of the book, to
see how much the consumer can absorb price increases simply
on catastrophic news.*
Both countries like Libya and Yemen and even Egypt are not
big players in the oil exporting game. The Suez Canal didn't
pose a threat as of yet to the transportation of oil tankers.
Yet in a matter of days, prices of commodities are going
upward even if the supply and production and reserves have
not been tampered with. *The finger again?*

FEBRUARY 23-20011-(EST) CNN News

Turmoil continues in the disfranchise countries as Iran's war
ship parades in the Suez Canal.
Tunisia has joined the unrest countries and creates a war zone
atmosphere. Bahrain is still in a crusade momentum as Egypt
celebrates its victory.
Iran's provocation did rattle the oil markets. Nothing like a
warship to create woes around the world.
Brent Crude Oil future at 110.5 + 4.32%
Gas F   913.0 + 2.24%

Heating Oil F. 288.030 +3.15%
Gas (RBOB) F 268.67 +3.25%
WTI F 98.110 + 2.82%
Silver –oz. 33.67 + 2.49%
Commodities that were up recently were *down* like Cotton-
Sugar- Oats and Rice and the US stock market.

The last report (02-21-2011) by EIA. doe. Gov. on retail gas
prices doesn't show significant increase in retail gas prices in
the US at $3.24gal.

Fuel Gage Report AAA.com reports retail gas prices at
$3.194gal. *no* significant change from a week ago or a month
ago, at $3.17gal and $3.11 gal.

Even Iran's leader calls Gadhafi's statement, ''an action
outrage.''

While there is no shortage of action creating havoc in the
Middle East where the world is keeping an eye on, as of yet,
there is no threat to oil flow, supply or reserve.

Nomura Securities published a statement saying that oil could
reach $220. bl. in its worst case scenario.

This is the kind of statement that gets people react and panic.
Of course it is the agitation going on in the Middle East that
propels oil prices, but it is more the ''insecurity'' or the
''unknown'' factor that froths over creating ''uncertainties''.

In reality, from one day to the next, there is no change in oil
supply, no change in oil reserves, no change in gasoline supply
and no change in American companies operating peacefully at
home. Unless there would be a fire at an American oil
company, destroying supply and production facilities, which
would give factual reasons of stock going down and oil going
up.

As I mentioned before, markets thrive on uncertainties and
chaos.

15.00 PM EST.

The threat is now real. Libya reduces its export of 0.5 million
BB/day. In total, Libya produces 1.6mbb/day and export

61

1.2mbb/day to Europe. One pipeline has been shut from Libya to Italy (Greenstrean) and some of it port has been shot down. Since we have to take this on a world market scale, Saudi Arabia told they will fill the gap. The only thing it would not be of the same quality. (Source: Petroleum Economist)

FEBRUARY 24-2011 E.S.T   (CNN News.)

As the world turns in disgruntled countries, gas prices in North America are showing its ugly head by rising gas at the pump. In Montreal, Canada, the price of gas increased in the last 24 hours of 10%, according to CTV news, at $1.264 liter. When asked to people filling up their gas tank, they say; ''this has nothing to do with the crisis in Libya since there is plenty of gas here at this moment. The oil companies are simply gauging, profiting from the crisis. ''
I couldn't agree more since Libya doesn't sell crude oil to North America. (Minimum in the US) Most of its exports goes to Italy and the rest of Europe. The other thing is that Saudi Arabia said it is capable of filling the gap. Let's keep in mind what I wrote on yesterday that Libya produces about 1.6 to 1.8 mbb/day and export about 1.2mbb/day. It is a small player in the world arena.
The NY Mercantile Index rose to $103.41 a barrel and the Brent Future rose to $119.79.
On the Bloomberg news this morning with Charles Maxwell from Weeden. Co, a senior analyst said: ''that the crisis in Libya today affects a small portion of the oil supply. There is a 5mbb / day in the system and most countries can crank up more as Saudi Arabia said.''
Even OPEC leader, Abdalla El-Badri said that a $100.00 barrel is a good price where economies can get out of the recession completely. Mr. Maxwell said that today's price is fair at $100.00 a barrel. Mr. El-Badri mentioned: '' if finance

ministers all over the world are worried about inflation by oil prices, they should do something about it since they make more money than we do on a barrel of oil.''

In a Canadian perspective, it is true that taxes play a major role in the gas prices and we are oil net exporters as well. We export about 1.0 mbb/day the US. Needless to say that governments make more money as well when prices are high. Who is left out to dry? The consumer. *Here is the finger one more time.*

The US government said that it will increase its reserve or stockpile of oil, thus increase in demand.

Bloomberg Commodities Index:
Brent Crude Oil Future $113.75 barrel +2.5%
Gas &Oil (ICE) F. 930 + 17.50 %
Heating Oil Future 292.63 +2.14%
Gasoline (RBOB) Future 275.35 +3.86%
WTI Future 99.20 +1.10%
NY Mercantile Index 99.53 (02-24-2011 noon, EST)

Agricultural commodities were practically all down.

I guess that money (speculators) is going into the oil markets and out of the agricultural commodities' market.

I would be obdurate and unyielding of me to say that there are no reasons to panic and all is well under the oil drum. Of course political crisis has its economic devastation when people stop working and abundant pillage is done to the infrastructure and its production and wants to overthrow the present government. But we are not there yet, not yet to justify an increase at the pump. *This is my qualm about instant price hikes in North America.*

As I mentioned, markets move on anticipation and not actual daily facts. I'm not surprise to see the future's market peak in response to the Middle East crisis but surprised only to see it increasing at ''my gas pump'' where I live.

Of course since the turmoil is spreading like wild fire to Algeria, where it could become as Libya's level, would be cause for concern, being a bigger producer. When one looks at the major OPEC producers being Saudi Arabia, Kuwait and Iran and Iraq, only Saudi Arabia is stable, thus bringing negative possibilities for the region. Nigeria is also a major player (the fifth US importer) in the oil export business where supply is safe for now.

Since Gadhafi is not wavering in his position, I don't see that things are eventually going to settle down. It is going to get worse before it gets better for Libya.

Time will tell if this apocalyptic view of the Middle East is warranted.

FEBRUARY 25-2011-(CNN News)

I think it is the Canadian Oil & Gas companies that are on drugs, not the Libyan people.

Gasoline in Montreal rose again to $1.33 /liter, the highest in the country. Toronto gas prices are much lower. It is public opinion that ''we don't have anything to do with Libya,'' remember that we are an exporting country!

US gas prices are rising as well. Feb.-21-2011 at $3.29gal. from $3.21gal. on Feb.-07-2011.

The US does import from Libya but a very small amount. Obama said that it can override the amount by reserves. Saudi Arabia is filling the gap, as previously said.

From a video interview on CNN with Professor Jeremy Siegel, a professor at Wharton school says; ''it is a blow up hype because the reality is that the actual total supply as not changed unless we see unrest in Saudi Arabia.''

Of course it is anticipated fear of seeing the oil price at $150.00 a barrel if political turmoil would spread all over the regions of the Middle East.

A reminder that Libya produces only 2% of world production and is a small exporter to the US.
Algeria produces 4% of world production.
Iraq produces 6% of world production.
Oil is 50% of the gasoline component and it does take time to be refined and be distributed. Is there isn't enough gasoline in the system to fill our tanks for a while even if worse comes to worse? The gas at my station was ''physically there'' two weeks ago. Why pay more? If not for companies gauging.
I think I made my point by following the crisis in the Middle East and local or North America's gas prices at the pump where instant increases in prices of gasoline are on the back of consumers and profiting North American oil companies. I really think that they have been gauging on the crisis, *giving us the finger.*
With the certainty of a civil war in Libya and other Middle East countries escalating tumult, and in Africa, the price of crude oil is doomed to go up regardless of actual damage to reserves and production.

Bloomberg Energy Future Index;
Brent Crude Future at $111.20 down from yesterday.
Gas Oil F (ICE) USD/MT- $917.75 down from yesterday
Heating Oil   (USD/gal. $287.73 down from yesterday
Gas (RBOB) $271.57 down from yesterday
WTI $96.99 down from yesterday.
Agricultural commodities were relatively stable and livestock as well. The only food commodity which was showing an increase was Rough Rice (CWT) at $14.11 +2.21%.
Obviously there is profit taking in these markets. Speculators love crisis, creating movements on markets.

FEBRURARY 26-2011 CNN News
Closing Friday was upward again on all energy commodities and the Natural Gas Future Index rose 3.43%

Agricultural Future Index where up from the previous day. Corn and cotton, wheat and soybeans were up over 3.0% as well as rough rice. Soybeans Index was up 4.0%

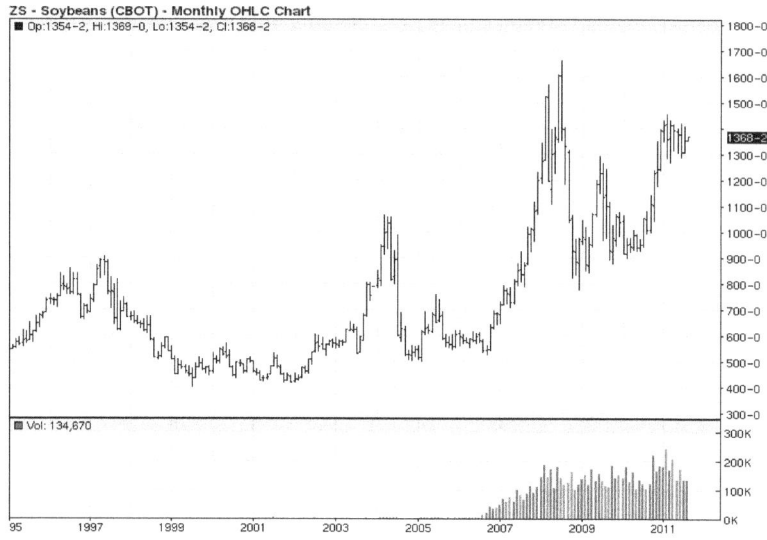

Precious metal futures were down a shade and livestock futures were up slightly.

Iraq as join the pillage by attacking an oil refinery and setting fire to it. Iraq is a major oil producer but this particular plant was a gasoline refinery plant. I don't think there is any export of gasoline, just the crude oil.

Côte D'Ivoire is also showing unrest and accounts for 4 deaths in its revolution.

The UN and U.S and Canada want to apply sanctions against the Gadhafi's regime if he doesn't step down which is unlikely. He does have a following and thinks he can win this with his partisans. The footing of a long civil war is set since neither party will comply for the other.

THUSDAY MARCH FIRST 2011-CNN News

Monday's market closed at a modest high for most energy futures indices and agricultural indexes were relatively stable except for cotton and sugar, up 3.66% for cotton and down 2.82% for sugar. Silver is still going upwards to $34.24, 1.26% increase.

Bloomberg's interview with Jim Rogers from Rogers Holding says that the oil prices increase is justified because Saudi Arabia is not going to increase production in order to fill the Libya's gap in export as Gadhafi's denial of insurgence continues. In the last TV interview, Gadhafi seems that he needed more to spend a few hours with Dr. Phil than his army general to accept what was going on in his country.

Energy Index

Brent up 1% to 112.9

Gas Oil 939.0 up .35%

Heating Oil 296.8 up 1%

Natural Gas 4.03 down

Gas RBOB 291.58 up .80%

WTI 97.8 up 0.84%

NY CRUDE $99.58

Agricultural Index

Oat future down 1.12% and Rough Rice 1.20%

No major moves in livestock.

National Inflation Association predicts hyperinflation this year in food prices as it has been for the last two years. Most are attributable to climate changes and China's growth. Arab countries say that inflation is imported from North America and North America blames China.

Recap of this month retail gas prices: Regular-average.
US in dollars/ gallon.
2/14/2011   2/21/2011   2/28/2011   Change week   Change in a year

$3.140 $3.189 $3.38
$0.194 $0.681
Source: EIA. doe. Gov.

CDN in dollars/liter (Montreal)
2/01/2011   2/09/2011   2/15/2011
2/25/2011
126.9 litre   125.4   126.4
133.4
Source: Gasticker.com
Canadian prices are lower elsewhere since Quebec his heavily taxes by the provincial government.

MARCH SECOND 2011- CNN NEWS

I am curious to see if the US warships getting closer to Libya are going to create a surge in oil prices as Tripoli faces protestors?
Brent Oil F   115.77 USD/bbl.
Gas Oil F   959.25 USD/MT
Heating Oil 303.11 USD/gal.
Natural Gas 3.87 USD/MMbtu.
Gasoline RBOB 300.56 USD/Gal.
WTI100.42 USD/bbl.
NY Mercantile   100.52USD/bbl.
Cotton #2 at 200. USD/lb. and Sugar # 11 at 30.115 USD/lb. and Soybean Oil 58.25 USD/T
Silver F 34.84USD/oz.
The rest are relatively stable and livestock as well.

MARCH THIRD (CNN News)

The mayhem continues in Yemen as protestors want obstinately governmental changes. Tripoli seems quiet but war is afoot as people flee to Tunisia. American retail gas price touches $3.40 nationwide.

The UN reports a 2.2% increase in grain, dairy products and meat cost for the month of February. See page 241 for details of the monthly Index increase. Food increase is blamed on Russia's drought and ban on the export of grain.

Yesterday's close on the energy index was slightly down as the money move back to equity stocks. Agricultural indexes were up except for sugar and soybean Oil index which were up considerably in the past few weeks.

See the monthly index report (page 241) for today's prices.
Source: Bloomberg Commodities.

Comment: I don't see why there should be an increase in grain and dairy in North America based on Russia's refrained export. We (US & Canada) have plenty of grain and dairy products. I'm sure we don't import those commodities. Why are indexes up?

SATURDAY'S CLOSE FOR THE WEEK-March 5-2011.

Most Energy Commodities closed upward from a monthly close report on March 3: (see page 210)
Brent crude at 115.97
Gas &Oil F at 969.0
Heating Oil F. 308.93
Natural Gas F. 3.809
Gas (RBOB) 304.64
WTI at 104.42
Most Agricultural Commodities closed upward with substantial gains (more than 1%) in:
Wheat F. to 832.25 a 1.06% gain
Wheat F. 928.5 a 1.12% gain
Lumber B/F 322.5 a 2.32% gain
Soybean Oil 59.48% plus 1.21%

Silver oz. at 35.32 plus 2.91%
No major increase in livestock.
Source: Bloomberg Commodities future Index.-March 5-2011

We all know by now what causes the price increase of energy
commodities. Nothing like street demonstrations, fires,
killings, tanks and warships in oil producing countries to rattle
people's faith and create uncertainties around the globe. My
concern is to watch closely what is done physically to oil
reserves, oil production and transportation, not to report the
news. We hear even if we want to or not what is going on in
the Middle East. Like I stated before, there are no physical
threat but only a potential threat. This is where the hype comes
from, juiced up by the media as we keep a scornful eye at the
gas meter at our gas station.
Even if we see a crude oil increase and agricultural
commodities increase, as of today, I don't see physical harm
or destruction done on crops and oil reserves. *Even if there is
enough chaos to worry about, who is pocketing the extra
profits on those increases? Yes, the major oil companies, the
speculators and the big producers of agricultural
commodities. Who is going to pay for that very soon? We are.*

MARCH- 8 -2011-CNN NEWS AND BLOOMBERG NEWS

As the WTI touches 105.02 at 12.30 EST, the Middle East
countries are continuing their belligerent attacks worrying the
world about a shortage of oil to produce gasoline.
Since last week, gasoline in the US has increased 13.7 cents a
gallon to $3.52 gal for regular- average. (Source: EIA. doe.
Gov.). and a $1.20 to $1.33 CDN/L in Canada.
Seeing thanks and fighting aircrafts near oil reservoirs is not
reassuring the market of future supply of oil. Even Gaddafi
seems to be oblivious to depleting reserve since he mentioned
that he would blow up reserves if he has too.

The US involvement would not appease things since we would be facing an international war, so to speak. Saudi Arabia's troupes are on the move which bring the major player into the picture. As things escalate, we are approaching more and more to the possibility that shortage will occur since world production is 85.5Mb/day and consumption is about 87.4Mb/day. Demand is rising since most companies and countries want to increase their stock. The world market is tight and the Middle East's convulsions are a disruption to the stability of oil prices. The Suez Canal was a concern but it was closed for only one day.

I can't shake out of my head why a producer of less than 2% of the world oil supply should affect us or the gasoline prices in North America in a short period of time. It takes 50% of oil to produce gasoline, some say 60% and there is a 5-8Mb / day in the system plus the reserves and both Canadian and U.S imports very little (zero for Canada and a small percentage for the US) from Libya. I know I've said it many times, and I guess I just don't accept it. Vailed by total obduracy, I can't conceive this when Canada is the second in oil reserves in the world after S.A. and the 6th or 7th producer in the world.

One aspect which I forgot to underline is why people are so upset by the increase of gas prices is that the industry is by nature and historically an *oligarchy* by structure. In other words it is controlled by very few and very large companies, either publicly owned or government owned.

From the exploration, to production, to refining, to distribution and retail products, all steps are in control of very few major names like EXXON, BP Oil, CHEVRON, ROYAL DUTCH SHELL and TOTAL.SA and CONOCO PHILIPS. About 40% of production goes on the open market.

It seems like it is the tail wagging the dog since the minority of production (40% open markets) is responsible for the price increase of rest 60% of production which is held and exploits the ''market increased'' escalating to high prices.

The large pool of capital needed to exploit and distribute oil pushes away entry in the market.

This is why this *oligopolistic* hand frustrates consumers, thinking that they have been ''had,'' once again unnecessarily when prices go up.

Remember that the best profitable year was 2008 for these major Oil companies when crude oil reached a peak of $147 barrel on markets.

As far as today, the stock market is stealing money out of commodities, investing in the oil companies to balance our lost at the pump.

MARCH 9- 2011 CNN & BLOOMBERG News

Since I have been tracking oil and gas prices since the Egypt crisis and Tunisia from February first, I don't really know what would spur prices to go up apart from a shortage of supply. Since there hasn't been a physical shortage of supply it is only psychological shortage, or speculators drumming up a little movement. Even Mr. S. Ghanem of National Oil Corporation of Libya said on March 3, that there is no shortage of oil and if there was, we can increase supply when the NYMEX was at $91.53

Higher oil prices mean higher food prices. Feeder Cattle was up to $1.37 on the CME.

One important factor which is not mentioned often is Oil Reserves. Newspapers seem to focus on production and consumption. There are millions of barrels in reserves. Yes millions.

And we have to pay more!!!

MARCH 10-2011 BLOOMBERG NEWS

Respite today on all fronts, even the stock market.

MARCH 11-2011 BLOOMBERG NEWS

When bad news is good news.-Japan's refinery on fire after an earthquake and tsunami is easing oil consumption and price and poor economic news from the US (jobless rate increase) contributes to easing in all markets even if Saudi Arabia is showing signs of unrest.

MARCH 14-RETAIL GAS PRICES
In the US $3.56 gal reg. average
(Source: EIA. doe.gov.)
In Canada $1.344 liter
Source: Gasticker. CA

MARCH 17-2011 12.45 EST-CNN & BLOOMBERG'S NEWS

All markets are up like a vengeance looking at China's warship near Libya and Saudi Arabia's troop in Bahrain as Japan's economic slowdown takes second place in world's worries. The substantial increase in energy (2% to 3%) markets and food commodity markets are a reaction of war like movie in the gulf. Is this going to translate in a rapid increase in gas and food retail prices throughout the world? We shall see.

From God's point of view, from way above, the planet seems to be approaching apocalyptic proportions seeing that our world is not short of belligerent behaviorism.

MARCH 18-2011-11.00 EST-CNN & BLOOMBERG NEWS
Release pressure on energy prices since Libya declared a cease fire on the rebels. Traders are going from energy to stocks and then agricultural commodities.

Agricultural commodities are pushing ahead today with Corn up 5%, Wheat (CBT) 4.47% and Wheat (KCB) 3.43% and Oat up 3.88%

Retail gas prices are computed every 7 days. Next report on the twenty first.

MARCH 21-2011 14.17 EST--CNN NEWS & BLOOMBERG NEWS& COMMODITIES

Brent Crude Oil F. at 115.37
Gasoline RBOB F. at 300.89
WTI at 102.39
NY Crude F. at 102.21
Cocoa F. at 3,212.0 USMT
Wheat (KCB) at $846.24
Corn at $676.5
Gold at $1432
Silver at $36.05
Retail gasoline in US; 3.562 USD/gal.   (EIA. doe. Gov)
Retail gasoline in Canada; $1.36.9 can /liter –at 23.00 hr. at
$1.236   (Gasticker.ca)

Since most eyes were on Japan's disaster, other unsettling news from other countries are influencing markets, Yemen, Saudi Arabia, Bahrain and Egypt and still Libya.
As I mentioned before, one country's disaster is someone else opportunity. It stands to reason that a major ''deconstruction'' have to be rebuilt eventually and life continues for the survivors. It is just the word I guess; ''opportunity,'' that is somewhat shocking, when one speaks of opportunities to make profits after a major devastation and thousands of lives lost. After a loss of 12% in Japan's stock market and major construction ahead, money will be going where the demand is; iron, steel, wood and communications companies where everything have to be reset; - re-connected.
Pragmatism is for the hard skin not the histrionic type.

I think investors in the futures market realized that the world economies are going to grow despite the slowdown in Japan and are pushing agricultural commodity prices higher.

As far as oil prices are concerned in the short term, investors and speculators have come to grips that Libya's production is only 2% of the world production and only 3% of US imports and production have not been tempered with in any significant way. The long term outlook is still on the rise since demand and supply is thigh. They say that world's production has reached a peak and looking at the population growth and China's economic growth, it is inevitable that prices are heading higher. I think in the next five years, electric cars are going to make an impact on gasoline consumption.

Air attacks on Libya by the UN coalition lead by the US doesn't forebode well for the future. It is a ''warning'' to Gadhafi to obey the no fly zone over the coast of Libya. I just hope this is not another Iraq.

Ironic that the coalition is flying over the ''no fly zone'' to ''bomb Libyans'' to refrain Gadhafi to fly and bomb Libyans!!!

MARCH 24-2011-CNN NEWS and BLOOMBERG and LOCAL.

As the ''warning'' by the coalition turns into a real war in Libya and the baby steps by the Canadian Jet brigade involvement from ''jet escort'' to launch on ammunition on barracks

brings the future's market to an all-time high.

Brent C F. at $115.70

WTI at $106.02

Silver at $38.05

Gold at $1446

Sugar # 11 at 27.53 plus 3.57%

Wheat F   at 848 up 2.17%

Wheat F (CBT) 732.75 up 2.59%

Oat F. 344.75 up 1.55%

The big debate is to ''who'' is going to take the lead in the coalition with evidence that the US doesn't want to because it doesn't look good. They don't want to appear that it is a war going on between the West and the Middle East. Politicians insist that the situation is ''not'' the same as Iraq's beginnings hoping that assaults will bare its fruit early and stop Gadhafi in his tracks. Even if the coalition is backed by the Arab League Council and other countries,

a jet attack is a sign of war. If it sounds like a war, (boom, boom) if it looks like a war, (bang, bang) it must be a war. There is no gasoline price increase in North America as of today but I'm sure they will be one soon.

I know a way to save on fuel; STOP FUELLING THOSE JETS.

APRIL 4-2011 CNN NEWS & BLOOMBERG NEWS

When good news is bad news and bad news is bad news. Since the release of US unemployment figure from 8.9% to 8.8%, inflation fear turns out its ugly head by pushing the Brent Oil future index and the WTI at record highs.

Brent crude at $118.70 (now at 119.80 at 12.00 EST) and WTI at $107.94

Gadhafi's strikes are making waves as well. The hopes of a ''bomb and run'' approach to settle things are looking pretty slim by now. There is no question even with the change in command of the NATO coalition, there is a full war going on in Libya even if the US was hoping that a few bombs would scare off Gadhafi and make him retaliate for good. No such luck.

The inflation fear is an over-reaction to say the least. A zero point 1 % (0.1%) doesn't create an economic boom, long way from that. Why is it mentioned in the papers that this is a premise for inflation? To help traders?

Banning food imports from Japan in case of radiation does create shortage and thus inflation. But I don't think that would cause an *immediate* price hike. We will know in a month or two if is the case.

APRIL FITH 2011 LOCAL NEWS

It didn't take long that retail gasoline prices in North America of being pushed up. I just got wind on TV that in Montreal, regular gas just went up to $1.39 liters. Even the Canadian dollar being over par from the US doesn't seem to help. The last price was on March 21 at $1.37 liter.

We will confirm officially retail prices when they are published from our regular source.

APRIL SIX-2011 CNN-E NEWS &BLOOMBERG NEWS-LOCAL GAS PRICES

Whenever Gadhafi make some gains in his war, the oil prices go up. Now sitting at $122.79 for the Brent Crude and $108.55 for the WTI (see Index page 241) is an all-time high and local and US gasoline as well, $3.684 /US gal. and $1.394 /liter for Montreal. (Official prices)

Predictions of higher energy prices are manifesting since people still worry about the shortage. Most specialists agree that the main reason is that oil production has reached a plateau of 87.4 million barrels a day and demand is slowly increasing toward 90 million barrels a day. I've stated world production and demand before and the numbers vary a bit but by in large, we reached production peak. Demand will be curtailed at $120 a barrel and $4.00 gallon based on history and the saying of Mr. T. Bone Pickens, a geologist billionaire.

We will have to see about that one if those prices will be an "economy choker" or not. Some are skeptical that countries and particular Saudi Arabia can increase oil production either to fill the shortage Libya is creating, if any, and the world supply in general. Have we really reached world maximum production? And the demand is not far behind or at par.

As far as agricultural commodities are concerned, demand and supply seem to be tight as well on all fronts. The market is in equilibrium but sensitive to climate change and effects on supply like radiation on food from Japan. According to Greg Smith, a commodity trader, we eat what we produce.
On the financial side, governments are worried about inflation and wonder if stimulus are still needed or "ride" the recovery without it. Will QE3 happen in June? The recovery GDP has been lowered from 3.0% a year to 2.5% a year for 2011. China's central banks have raised interest rates of 1.25% fearing inflation. Will US follow?
The ECB is expected to raise interest rates today by .25 basis points and is expected to raise it again this year up to a full point.

I've touched the subject before about energy and food production *worldwide* and inflation as well and still remain skeptical because of speculation and hoarding and the media spreading the apocalyptic news.
This being said, we are experiencing historical events around the world where a dozen countries are in a civil war, facing runaway prices as we worryingly trying to see the future.
We are looking at elections in the States and in Canada.
The leaders are shown discontent from all sides by the population about their leadership and governments. People are rallying for just about anything all around the world even in stable countries.

APRIL 8- 2001-FRIDAY'S CLOSE APRIL
7TH.BLOOMBERG NEWS

Energy commodities went flying after the ECB raised its key
rate by 25% basis point to 1.25%.
Brent Crude F. to 126.65 up 3.24%
Gas F (ICE)   1,048.25 up 2.69%
Heating Oil F. 331.97 up 3.55%
Natural Gas $4.01 minus 0.31%
Gas RBOB F. 325.07 up 2.33%
WTI F   112.79 up 2.26%
Some agricultural commodities as well;
Wheat F CTB 832.25 up 2.87%
Soybean F   1396   up 2.23%
Oat F 402   up 5.24%
Soybean Oil F   60.39 up 2.46%
Silver to $40.68 oz. up 2.67%
Euro up 1.7% to $1.4483 USD.

It is clear that Europe is running at two different speeds,
Germany leading and Ireland, Greece and Portugal and Spain
lagging.
Rising rate tells us the economy is growing too fast and
booming while some are in great need of a bailout. The rising
interest rate is putting oil on the fire for the lagging economy
since it puts flexible mortgage at a higher rate and government
debt payment at higher cost, thus putting the brakes on any
chance of recovery.
Since Mr. Trichet the president of the ECB thinks there is
inflation in Germany coming soon, markets went flying on all
fronts pushing commodities futures' at record highs.
Making an average judgement about Europe seems to be a
wrong move at the wrong time.

It was the main concern to begin with when the European Union was created, creating the EURO, a common currency for all countries, the rich as well as the poorer countries. Rich and poor might be an overstatement but we can use more industrialized and ''slower'' economies are much smaller economies than Germany.

Does this mean that the US will raise rates?

Since the US Treasury is pondering about QE3, it is unlikely that an increase will occur even if another round of stimulus is needed.

Inflation is the enemy number one for all governments but as far as I'm concerned, I rather live in a booming economy with inflation as opposed to a recession or deflation.

APRIL 16-2011-BLOOMBERG NEWS

Since our last reckoning of commodity prices on April 8th prices went soft on crucial commodities on the futures market influencing the spot market.

Brent Oil F at $123.45
Gas Oil F at $1,027.250
Heating Oil F $322.42
Natural Gas F $4.20
Gasoline RBOB $328.92
WTI at $109.66
Gold oz. at $1486.0
Silver at $42.57

APRIL 18-2011 - BLOOMBERG NEWS. 12.00 noon EST.

S&P negative outlook but not the actual downgrading of the AAA rating for US debt managed to push Gold and Silver to a *new time high* and the stock market retreat as Wheat Futures gain close to 4% higher on markets.

Gold is at $1496

Silver at $43.37
Wheat F (CBT) at $810.750
Wheat F (KCB) at $906.50

APRIL 20 NOON E. S. T-BLOOMBERG NEWS

The S &P's dim view on the budget deficit is still taking its
toll on gold and silver as investors and speculators are shying
away from the dollar. Gold reached $1504 mark and Silver at
$45.
Some forecasters must be jubilant today, the ones that
mentioned that Gold could reach $2,000. and Silver at $50.
Oz.
The future will tell but those marks are important because they
are psychological benchmarks.
The Yuan keeps going up as well as other Asian currencies. Is
the specter of having the Yuan as THE international currency
getting real?
Spain has been finding takers on auction on bond issue. Price
went up after the issue to yield 5.47%.

APRIL 21-12.00 EST BLOOMBERG NEWS.

Greek bonds take a tumble as yield reaches 14.93% on its 10
year note. Its 2 year note reaches yield of 23.25%.
Portuguese bonds 10 year note reaches 9.58% and 2 year note
11.52%
German 10 year note yield at 3.26% and 2 year note at 1.76%
Frances 10 year notes yield 2.92% and 2 year note at 1.93%
According to EFFA compilations, all European bond markets
lost some grounds this year including the Ireland bond market.
The US yields are stable accepting Obama's deficit cut
proposal.

Gold and silver managed to slightly go up again over the psychological benchmark.

Every time I hear that a country is in the possibility of not being able of honoring its debt gives me some kind of trepidations probably because I think of the civil servants who's pay might be in jeopardy and everything will fall to pieces afterwards.

Influenced by the media, no such dire situation will occur until there is a debt restructuring possibility in the offing. As I mentioned before, they (IMF) reset the debt, or devalue the currency and brace for better years ahead.

Even some large cities like New York went technically bankrupted (with no currency to devalue) but were bailed out by the State and the Federal governments a few years back. Any Governmental assets are not ''repossessable'' and it is simply a matter of adjusting the books and life goes on.

Sure, countries like Greece have to borrow at extremely high price, but by in large everything is temporary until a better solution is found and better economic times are back.

Is all of this, (Debt and payments) is just a play on words and profit one community only; the secondary market players which are speculators using fiat money?

One thing for sure is that trading bonds, stocks and currencies doesn't affect a nation's wealth. Gains or losses are not creating or diminishing wealth. Banks and funds and individuals might feel richer or poorer in a giving time, but those assets with fiat money are not real assets and real wealth. Like the book value of a stock on the market is ephemeral to say the least since only demand and supply will determine the break-up value of real assets. If you're trying to sell obsolete trains when nobody wants them, the asset or book value is quite fictitious. Ratios and break-up value are inconsequential to value or wealth.

If you believe Las Vegas really exist, it does. If you don't, it doesn't exist. After all, it was a pure creation of a mobster in a place where nothing lived, a hundred miles to the nearest toilet. It was a mirage that came through for some but it is all what it is; a mirage. There is the hotel called the Mirage and it is not for nothing. Even the winners of gambling are soon departed of their winnings on foolishness since it is not money earn, not real. Owners of casinos which are dwelling in millions up or down every day, have become oblivious to money since it might dissipate the next day.

The middle class is trying to get rich but to no avail since the odds are against them. The super-rich is trying endlessly to blow money away just trying to beat the odds or to be able to tell that they lost millions and proud to be able to laugh about it. Losers are just as proud as the winners. Simply an exercise in futility.

APRIL 23-2011-CNN & BLOOMBERG NEWS.

The close of markets yesterday had reached an all-time high for silver at $46.07 while gold sustained a price of $1503.80. The dollar weakens at the same time.

The war in Libya is reconfirmed by introducing the ''drones'' to fight Gadhafi's forces as Governor McCain makes a commitment by showing up in Libya.

Syria's turmoil is growing into a civil war as well as in Nigeria. Nothing to appease prices of oil and pushing commodity prices higher.

In the last six months, the Fuel Oil Index grew by 37.2% and 34% in the last twelve months.

Energy Index grew by 15.5% in the past month. The Food Index grew at a rate of 2.9% in the last twelve months.

Retail gas prices remained high, at $3.844 a gallon. (4/18/2011) and $1.39 liter in Canada (4/11/2011)

The S&P probable decrease in US AAA Bond rating didn't have its affect since yields on the 2 year note declined to .66% and the 10 year note to 3.40%.

With Obama's cut and decrease in the budget did influence the S& P's bluff.

Two years hence is a long time and a scolding doesn't suffice to make a large difference.

I think it is inconceivable that the US rating be changed. Downgrading was done already on the currency market against other currencies.

^CHFUSD - Swiss Franc/U.S. Dollar (FOREX) - Daily OHLC Chart

APRIL 26-2011-BLOOMBERG NEWS

The US dollar has loss against the Euro six days in a row. The USD is 0.6849 Euro and the Euro is worth $1.4623 USD. (April 26-2011)

Silver is down a bit after touching $50.00 presently at $45.175 Investors are taking a break from looking more at the Royal wedding preparations coming up.

APRIL 28-2011-BLOOMBERG NEWS-CNN NEWS

Markets are oscillating while the Royal wedding takes the
front stage.

Brent F. $125.38	Gold at $1538.80
Nat gas F. $4.47	Silver at $48.90
Gasoline RBOB $344.52	EU/USD 1.4788
WTI at $ 112.85	DOW at
12733.60	
	S&P 500 at
1357.26	
	NASDAQ at
2865.42	

While there is still unrest in the Middle East, unrest by
tornados and floods in the US, and unrest in Washington about
possible inflation and economic data, the Royal wedding
hiatus takes center stage as people wants to think positive at
least for a day and creating a relief from watching world
disasters. I just hope there won't be any lives lost on the 29 of
April.

RECAP OF PREMISE

In order to align my thoughts about the objectives of this book,
I'm waiting by following the course of events, the rapid
inflation which some people predict, uncontrollable food
increase as we (the world) are expected in 2011. Not
anticipating, but merely bracing for it.
Are food shortages and oil shortages are real or manipulated?
Is QE 2 is the worst thing a government ever did? Is zero
interest rate on Fed funds is the thing to do?
The US Government has been known to raise rates in a
recession, making the worst mistake of monetary policy in
history. Is it making another mistake by keeping rates low this

time around for so long as other countries are raising rates after QE2?
As if the downfall of the US dollar wasn't inflationary enough.
Where are the policies of keeping a strong US dollar?
The future is a nebulous thing for all of us. For some, it is more hopeful, for some, it is with a little more gloom built into it.
Time will tell.

MAY SECOND-CNN NEWS-BLOOMBERG NEWS

It is a bit of a shame to rejoice when somebody dies, but the death of Osama bin Laden is a turning point, at least it brings some closure to the victim's siblings of September 11.
It makes the US representatives happy that is a well-recognized strike against al Qaeda.
Gadhafi's son has succumbed to the same fate.
Nevertheless, it sounds a bit barbaric that we, (the West) are keeping score at our enemies by being glad of life lost; in other words, killing people. To me, it proves that civilization, if one can still call it that had made very few steps forward to being ''more civilized.'' Men were fighting against each other since the human race began, creating a history of bloody wars, one after the other, like wild animals and still persist to this day.
I'm not overly chagrined by O. bin Laden's death since he is responsible for many deaths by organizing attacks on North America (9/11) and around the world. When one lives by violence, one dies by violence. As the saying goes; Live by the sword, die by the sword.

Back at home, Bernanke's first speech was somewhat conservative not to introduce panic among consumers so that the recovery won't be disturbed from its ailing past. Calling the rapid price increase on food and gas, TRANSITORY, is wishful thinking at best.

Since early February until today, May second, (4 months) price has increased (see Monthly Index at the end) for the Crude Oil of 25%,

WTI, of 25%,

Coffee of 22%

Corn of 12%

Gold of 16%

Silver of 62% and

Cattle of 8%

Gasoline retail in USD is at $3.963 gal. An increase in 4 months of: 29%

Gasoline retail in CDN is at $ 139.40 liter. An increase in 4 months of: 21 %

Some commodities went down and others remained stable. The USD lost 7% against the EURO in 5 months and all currencies have lost against Gold and Silver. If people buy precious metals to beat inflation or currency devaluation in the open market, they have succeeded but have also depressed the USD since Gold and Silver are denominated in USD.

US petrol oil stock, like EXXON, TOTAL, BP OIL, CHEVRON, have increase on the stock market of 20% because of their *most* profitable year.

Energy secondary markets have increased on there-own, and Oil Companies have profited to increase retail gasoline as well by the same percentage. We are given the *finger* again but it is ''lubricated.''

MAY THIRD-CNN NEWS-BLOOMBERG NEWS

Profits, profits, always for profits, being the most utilized word in financial communications.

As I mentioned yesterday the *good* year oil companies are having, picking our pockets steadily like it isn't their fault since the crude oil market keeps going up. They are supplying the ''MARKET'' with 40% of their oil finding allowing to trade. The 60% of it is being sold as gasoline to you. I've mentioned that before, the division of markets and users and again, they are benefiting from world's frenzy and speculators to pocket excess profits. Again, the royal finger for consumers.

Deutsche Bank faces a legal lawsuit from the US over mortgage lending from insurance programs through its affiliate company; Mortgage IT.
The big boys are at it again playing ''book tricks'' to look better in front of authorities.
One of the largest banks is skipping the rules, what is it left for us? Even after the trillion dollar bailout of US banks which many people think it was just a ''big fraud,'' we are not at the end of our misery yet.

Archer Daniels Midland Co. (ADM) the largest grain producers, is posting one of the largest increase in profits of 37% on grains for the third quarter. Sales have jumped 33% and operating profits on corn alone was up 96%. Who had this great idea to make ethanol with corn again?
Using food to make gasoline additive just sound simply incongruous.
They say that increase in demand is the reason prices are going up. Perhaps it is the profits that are going up based on the increase of retail prices? Just an idea.
I don't see an increase in demand for food products of over 30% in a given year. People just don't increase their food intake by that much even with an increase in population.
Again, we are given the *finger* as consumers are obligated to pay the increase in prices.

CINCO DE MAYO-MAY FIFTH-CNN NEWS & BLOOMBERG NEWS

The big news today is the decline of gold and silver prices. The markets are thinking that the recovery will be slow, very slow since jobless claims have rose of 43,000 from the previous month. Silver down by 8% today so far and gold by 2%. Since the Euro was down by the possibility of a rate increase by the ECB, the dollar was up in today's trading sessions.
In my ''market letters'' they are glad of what they predicted that silver was eventually going down.
I wouldn't quote Newton at this point, but what goes up must come down. Otherwise, it wouldn't be called a ''market.''
Remember, its take a seller and a buyer to make a trade.

MAY SIX-CNN & BLOOMBERG NEWS

When good news is bad news. After posting an increase in job growth of 244,000 in April,
Oil jumps (WTI) back over the $100 mark.
Markets are sensitive to economic news since everyone wonders if we are pulling out of recession or not when unemployment is still at 9%.
Retail gas prices are still going up as Crude oil is going down. T.V news reported Canadian prices in Quebec are $1.4600 a liter.
The Official US prices are still at $ 3.963 but in some areas they are over $4.00 gal.
We will wait for the published figure next week and try to find the reasoning behind the hikes.
MAY 10-2011-CNN NEWS & BLOOMBERG NEWS
Greece is still in dire straight giving the EURO a bit of a knock against the USD.

Bernanke's policy on QE2 seemed to have curtailed core inflation and easing liquidity into the market as US job creation is picking up. We see the tip of the submarine coming out of the water. The only thing is that Bernanke's figure on inflation seemed to be low particularly on food commodities where prices have risen considerably in the last two years. Now, one can buy a 4 pack of can beers for the same price you used to pay for a 6 pack not long ago. (CDN prices)

In my book it is a 33% price increase.

Why is it that US government still uses core CPI without food and energy and come up with an inflation rate of around 2.0%? The IMF reports US inflation at 3.6%

What do we have to worry about if it is not for food and energy?

I won't buy a tractor anytime soon but I will surely drive to buy my groceries.

MAY 11-2011-BLOOMBERG NEWS

The big news today is that US oil reserves have been raising, putting some relief on crude oil.

Brent at $113 down 3.84%

Gas Oil down 2.57%

Heating Oil down 2.97%

Gas RBOB down 7.52%

WTI down 4.79%

And Corn and Wheat are also down over 4.0% and Silver down 8.50%

The last retail prices of gasoline in the US (average-regular) is still at $3.96 gal. and in Canada, Quebec, Montreal-North has jumped last week at $146.90 litre. (Posted May 10)

I think oil companies profited from an oil leak in some western piping and decide that gas should go up from 07cents from $1.39 liter. Quite an increased for an oil leak that hasn't shown in inventory yet. I see the *FINGER AGAIN* from oil companies.

MAY 12-2011-BLOMMBERG NEWS

Markets are taking a respite on all fronts, from profit taking to changing our view on the US economy and thinking that oil prices have seen the high end and retail gasoline staying high. I'm glad to see that Mr. T. Boone Pickens, the oil billionaire had a good day when a Bill passed through Congress about accepting and favour the switch to natural gas fuel for trucks from diesel fuel. I think it is a first, of a great economic move against the dependency on OPEC oil. He thinks the US can save 2.5 MBD from this conversion and would cut imports by half. There is plenty of natural gas around and it is now cheap relative to oil and much cleaner than petrol. I think this a great stride for the US.

In regards to the tax break of big oil companies do have, it is time someone does something about it. Today, the Senate Finance Committee is meeting with the big corps CEO to cut the tax breaks or subsidies which sounds worst and more real than ''tax break'' to companies who are in fact controlling the world. I don't think there is much pity for big oil companies this time around.
Exxon Mobil reported a 69% increase first quarterly profit, the largest in 8 years, with a net income of $10.7 billion for the year. With a 29% increase in oil this year, Senator Charles Schumer, a NY Democrat doesn't see why subsidies should be given when the deficit is so large and the US dollar has declined so much in the past year, which makes life difficult for consumers.
When they speak, they weep.
Exxon's CEO Mr. Rex W. Tillerson said that if tax break are taken away, it will cost jobs and slow down the economy. Just for an exercise, if we take the salary and bonuses and stock

options and other little goodies of the top ten executives put together, cut it in half and see how much savings we can come with? That would be a start.

A company doesn't have to own 6 or 7 Lear Jets for their executives. (Saw this on TV.) (Sic)

Watching gold and silver going up at the expense of the US dollar and the talks that China wants to convert 1 trillion dollars, (its foreign reserve is 3 trillion) into gold made me wonder that if people, investors, banks, speculators like gold so much, why don't we return to the Gold Standard like it was before it was abolished in 1971?

I mentioned that to one of my neighbours just last week and I'm reading this week, May 11 on Bloomberg that Steve Forbes predicts that the Gold Standard will return in the next five years. One has to respect Steve Forbes, the financial billionaire.

When he speaks, people listen.

My feeling was good.

Only my neighbour who was listening didn't agree. Hum…..

FRIDAY MAY 13-2011-

It may be a good day to stay out of the markets.

SAT. MAY 14-2011

In my Wealth Wire Letter, they mentioned that US inflation **is at 8.8%** and Bernanke is still saying that core inflation is at 3.6% and we don't have a problem.

I really don't know why the Bureau of Labour Statistics publishes inflation rate without being seasonally adjusted with energy and food if it's not the reason, particularly now that oil and food is going crazy? And they try to calm us down by saying that it is only temporary. The core inflation figure takes so many figures into account *except food* and *energy* and come

up with 3.6% inflation. Since crude oil did increase of 29% which trickles down just about anything since energy is required for almost anything plus transportation. How can they segregate the rise of energy and food in the core inflation rate? Not only it is a right out lie, it is insulting to people when the price of food goes up almost daily. **The 8.8% inflation** is more believable because we can literally see it. DA!
The finger again.

MAY 16-2011. (My 14 cereals slice bread just went up by 6%)

I still don't understand why Governments publish CPI separately when it comes to Energy and Food. I know these commodities are fluctuating quite a bit at times and I guess there is wishful thinking it won't last long or won't affect the annual core inflation.
With numbers like 31.3% increase on fuel for the last twelve months ending in March (CPI Statistic Canada) and 18.9 % for gas for the last twelve months preceded by a 15.7% increase for the prior 12 months and energy in general went up 12.8% preceded by a 10.6% increase for the previous year. As much as the Canadian and the US core CPI is just at 3.1% in the last twelve months (without energy and food) is still published like everything is *UNDER* control.
With increases hikes like these, on food and energy, everything is *OUT* of control.
What do I care about if it is *not* food and gas? A price increase on Louis Vuitton's hand bags?
Bernanke says that energy price increases are temporary.
They are just beginning to trickle down into the mainstream of all products since it takes energy for almost anything, like I

stated before. What manufacturing product doesn't take
energy and if not manufactured, doesn't need transportation?
As I mentioned before, any loss of the US dollar on the
exchange rate to other currencies is also part of inflation. Since
Canada is the largest trading partner of the US (and vice versa)
the CDN gained 6.03% in the last twelve months as of May
18-2010.
(Source: OANDA Corp.)

See graph.

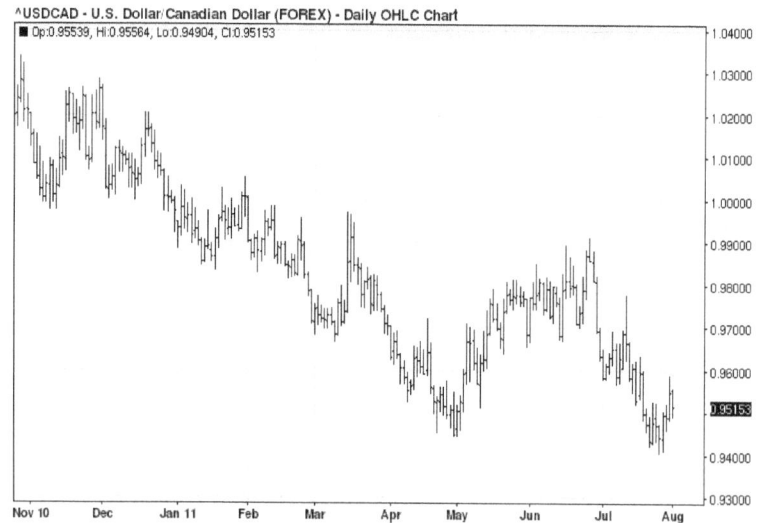

^USDCAD - U.S. Dollar/Canadian Dollar (FOREX) - Daily OHLC Chart

This 6.03% is on top of the declared inflation rate.
In relation to other currencies, the USD lost 22.14% against
the Suisse Franc,
and 14.96% against the Euro, 12.49% against the British
Pound. The only comforting aspect is that the Euro also lost
against the Suisse Franc of 10.50%.

The Suisse Franc is the strongest currency since the Bank has the most reserve of gold per capita.

What really sustains the USD is the price of oil which is traded in USD. If that wasn't the case the USD would have fallen considerably more.

I'm sure some bankers and the IMF are thinking of creating a basket of currencies for international trades for oil like they are presently using (SDR) for their own conversion of its members.

I'll reiterate the point that *gold* will eventually come back in an official backup of the US dollar or some other currency. This is why China is thinking of buying one trillion dollars of gold to eventually back up its currency which they want it to be used as an international currency exchange: besides, they don't want any more US debt securities.

QE3 might be coming at the end of June since the economy is sluggishly recovering. It does make expert jittery and looking dim at runaway inflation if it happens.

MAY 20-BLOOMBERG NEWS-

According to some experts like Marc Faber from the Gloom, Boom and Doom economic letter, he thinks the QE3 is inevitable since the result of the latest economic figures are slug- hiss. New housing sales are down, the secondary housing market is down, Philly Fed is down, which is the manufacturing report and growth for the last quarter was only 1.8%, leading indicators down 0.3%, consumers comfort down and so on.

Bernanke is ridding the time period he has left until June 30th by not committing of saying anything.

Albeit QE3 is viewed to be disastrous if it happens since QE2 did not create jobs, it only boosted the stock market and for instance, managed to double new IPO's like LINKED IN, in one day. The doubling of a stock in one day if proof that after accounting value of the IPO price is a guess work and speculators decided that wasn't the right price for its potential. It wasn't trading on P/E before and certainly not after doubling. What is the value of the stock? It is certainly not the market price as we can see.

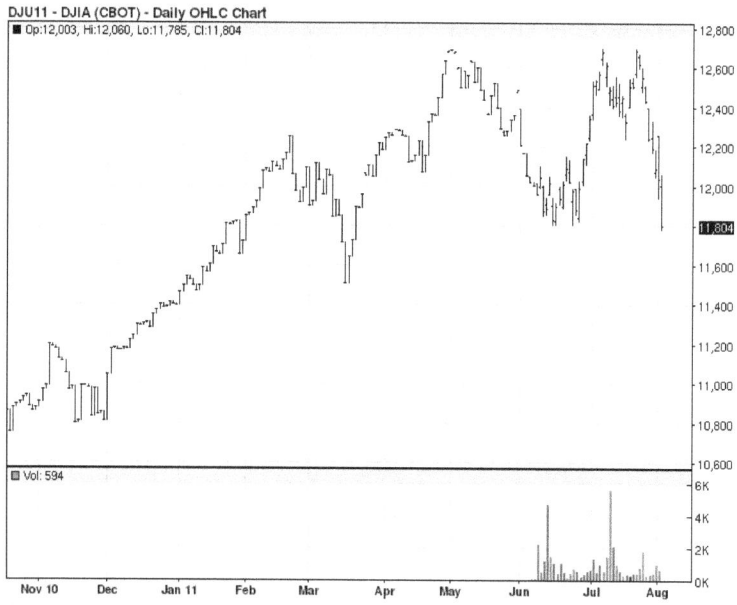

Unearned money from thrown in the market cannot be good for inflation.

A higher stock market doesn't create "Wealth" as I said before. Even if investors have bigger portfolios, they are not any richer since it is only paper, thus a fickle value of faith because secondary stock value is meaningless and labelled in fiat paper money which is losing purchasing power and its credibility around the world. We all know by now that values of these "assets" can lose a substantial percentage almost overnight.

Marc Faber predicts a correction of US stock shortly of 20%. He also thinks that rates should be at 5% to curb inflation and sustaining the dollar.

As far as I'm concerned, I rather keep my eyes on commodities and where those Ohio and Mississippi floods are going to affect farmland, crops and prices.

It is the first real factor that would affect supply that I've heard in a long time. I never believed that world food supply was so tight, influencing prices as they did.

Now that we have a little respite on energy prices, perhaps it will damper commodity prices a bit. We shall see!

MAY 23-2011-BLOOMBERG NEWS

Greece's debt is shaking the EURO on the currency markets and the stock market is shaken by the slow economic manufacturing rate in China. All commodities indices and stock indices are in red territory. The big question is; will the US raise rates soon?

Bernanke is looking at the economic performance and inflation and can't decide which one is unmoored to either benefit the economy or if the latter, will damper the possible growth.

The good news since crude oil prices are weakening, retail gas prices are sowing sign of respite by easing somewhat.

US May 23-2011 is $3.849 gal. a drop of .111 (EIA.doe/Gov.)

CDN Gasticker.com May 15 at $1.404 liter from $1.469 in Montreal North.

On May 12 at $1.460 a liter in Quebec City and May 17 at $1.285 liter in Toronto.

It doesn't go down as fast as it did going up and the decrease is not as significant as the decrease of crude oil. Eastern Canada pays much more than central and western provinces.

To the contrary, western states are more expensive than the East Side States.

MAY 24-2011 BLOMBERG NEWS- TIME: 12.00

The Markets have been going sideways since the rise of commodities Index yesterday based on Goldman Sachs recommendations. Waiting in the sidelines seems to be a quiescent period from negative economic news from the world around.

-Greek's debt is seemingly the horror story

-Fourteen U.K financial institutions are pegged at lower rating by Moody's

- Belgium's debt seems too big for refinancing

-Britain's budget in April has a the biggest shortfall ever

-China economic news is; slower manufacturing goods for last month

-Jobless rate in the US is up 43,000 to 474,000

-Is QE3 is going to happen? People wonder.

So, money doesn't know where to go except for hot IPO's like Yandex NV from Russia listed on Nasdaq was up 38% on the first day of trading.

Too bad this money wasn't used for real investments into the economy and created jobs!!!

MAY 30TH. 2011-BLOOMBERG NEWS.

As we get used to belligerent activity, the world is again preoccupied by Greece's debt.

Italy sold some 12 billion worth of debt a little higher than expected and Spain is scheduled to raise some debt on June 2. Greece's bailout is not done yet but the Canadian government pledged some help to the leader. Russia mentioned that it will lift the band on wheat export since European crops have been poor due to droughts and floods. Oil is weakened by a slowdown in the US economy.

It seems like everyone is on the sideline waiting for QE2 to end and see if there is going to be QE3 at the end of June.

Markets are going pretty much sideways.

Gasticker.com 05/27/2011 $1.384 litre from $1.35   A short relief.

E.I.A.doe/Gov. 05/23/2011 $ 3.849 from $ 4.014   An insignificant relief.

MAY 31-2011-BLOOMBERG NEWS

Things are back to normal; ''prices'' are going upwards.

The Brent Oil index is slowly surpassing the $115 mark to $116.36 and the WTI surpasses its threshold of the $100 mark to $102.63.

Saudi Arabia mentioned or admits that they are running out of oil. Apparently oil production peaked in 2006.

We are running out of cheap oil since we have to look further and deeper for it.

According to one oil company spokesman, ''we'' confusion as probable reserve as available reserve which is not the case. Oil in the ground is not reserves or inventory.

Lumber prices are up 3.77% due to Japan's strong demand for reconstruction.

All markets are up so as Gold and Silver, $1538. 90 and $38.515 respectively.

Greece's restructuring debt brings out one difficulty which is ''bank restructuring''. One cannot happen without the other. If Greece needs ''banking restructuring'', also does Portugal, the Netherlands and all of the European countries. A big task ahead.

JUNE FIRST-CNN NEWS & BLOOMBERG NEWS

All markets are down, seeing red with only a few exceptions like gold and silver.

Hampering economic news from China and the US are affecting possible sustainable growth.

I've heard it from the horse's mouth. Prince Al. W. bin Talal from Saudi Arabia said that he wants prices for oil to be between **$70. to $80.** a barrel which would be right for consumers and producers. The recent hikes were done by *speculators* and *the fear factor* that pushed demand for nothing.

Saudi Arabia spokesman said this before, that they want lower prices in order not to choke the economy. And they also said;
'' that if prices are too high thinking that it might contribute to inflation all over the world, Governments around the world can lower their taxes since they *make more profit* on a barrel of oil than *we do*.'' (Said this before)

Through that Governments make more money when prices are high.

Who is working for whom? *I see a finger at consumers*.

We seem to be totally pissed off at prices of $4.00 gal but maybe we should be content since they are, out of 170 countries analyzed, 147 countries are paying more than that and even double, plus $8.00 gal. (Converted).

By in large, I think speculators had a lot of fun so far this year profiting from the fear factor of political turbulence around the world.

Since economies and more so the US is not recovering as vigorously as we expected or want, it stands to reason that money is going in the wrong places not creating jobs, like the stock market and the increasing derivatives market, the culprit of the last recession. Wall Street as no shame of trying to come up with more derivatives like bundling Life Insurance policies and selling them to investors. It is ''déjà vue'' and warrants only another setback.

Mark Mobias of Templeton funds says that he is expecting a major correction in the stock market pretty soon and he's also not alone on this line of predictability.

Avid speculation always precedes busts. Isn't it what we see that the stock market is way ahead of the real economy? The doubling prices on new venture stock in one day?

JUNE FIFTH –BLOOMBERG NEWS

On our monthly take on commodities, most of them have receded from the February position. (See page 241) many reached a higher price but regain consciousness at lower levels.

On closing of June 3, I'm surprised to see some agricultural commodities going down like Oats, and Wheat and Lumber since the Japanese demand should be strong for lumber. Wool is up and corn and coffee from February prices. Most energy commodities have fallen back put are still up from the beginning of our watch of 15% or so.

I think the Chinese slower economic performance put a damper on some prices or at least it provided stability on others. Some analyst says that some metal prices like copper and silver might go down as much as 50%. It seems like a substantial bearish call from only an economic slowdown, taken the US anemic recovery.

The stock market has seen red this week where the money is going more in new IPO's which sounds better than existing stocks which had gone up considerably at a 45 degree angle on the chart since July 2010 to May 2011. Lots of money went in basic metals IPO's since it is up 32% and all IPO's were up 77% raising $ 17.3 billion. Will all this venture capital create jobs? Create wealth? When we don't see an easing of unemployment stuck at a stubborn 9%.

At least the Fed is doing something by appointing Paul Volker into a watch dog position on the Federal Deposit Insurance board with other top gun people to oversee the big banks and other semi-banks. Remember, the ones that were to ''big to fail!''

I've mentioned before that companies are getting so big that even analysts and Governmental Agencies like the SEC can't not follow what is actually going on because it is too darn complex. We need people that have been in those positions before to understand it all.

In Europe, the ECB president's J.C. Trichet has suggested a Finance Ministry to make countries comply with policies that will keep them out of bankruptcy. So far, the ECB doesn't have any legal pull to tell countries what to do. Seeing Greece closer to the financial cliff it sounds more like mandatory regulations are needed rather than just a suggestion.

George Papadreou is burning midnight oil to come to terms with the ECB and the IMF.

Some financial letters come up with suggestions that the US stock market is due for a major correction and others say that the second haft of this year should be good for US stocks. Take your pick.

As for myself, I see a major summer correction since the stock market has been *too* good so far without sustainable economic growth and then later this year, the last quarter, should demonstrate good performance. All these IPO's might create jobs after all.

Some big names like Mark Mobius, Jeremy Grantham and John Taylor, all big fund managers, are predicting a major correction. It would be easy to agree with them for the same reasons but since I'm not a follower, I agree for some simple reasons. I don't have charts and models to rely on, only good economic sense.

I remember in late 1987 when the stock market peaked and everybody was smoking cigars in the investment world but what struck me was that farmers were having difficult times. They were poor. To my disbelief, I realized that it was the same thing before the market crash in 1929. Speculation was the ''in game'' and farmers were suffering. Gee! That is not right!

So, I've deducted that in 1987 when things were literally flying, I said, this is going to come down like a rock in a sock sine our base economy, agriculture is down. And it did. The Dow went from 2650 to 1850, a 30% lost in a week. My broker friends were surprised that little old me made an accurate call when things were so great.

Today, June 8, 2011, I see the same thing. I see that money is going into the market by the bucket full and speculation on these hot IPO's while the man on the street is suffering from high food prices and are still having a hard time making ends meet, spending too much of their net income on food and rent. The farmers are not getting the income of the high food prices, the larger food transforming companies are and speculators. Gee! That is not right.

When I see extremes like this, from expensive Cuban cigar smoking to Spam eating, like I did 1987 and recalled my history of the 1929 crash, I see a stock correction since there is no wealth accumulating only speculation and the fundamentals are weak.

JUNE, 8- 2011-BLOOMBERG NEWS.

Everyone is watching Greece's canoeing in high financial waters. A rollover seems possible, said J.C. Trichet from the EU Bank.

Since Greece can't devalue the Euro unless they would go back to their own currency, a roll- over of old debt to new debt is the only way out. Since the Greek government does have some assets it can liquidate, those assets can re-balance the books and brace and hope for a quick economic turn- around. I hate to see that I was right saying previously that it is a matter of turning the clock on new debt and here we go again. The IMF and the ECB can't really seize the assets themselves and sell them to foreign interests. The only thing to do is changing the numbers on those bonds and lets' go back to eating Souvlakis and Tzatziki and drinking Retsina wine.
It's like the magician on a stage with a big saw and a woman lying in a box which he is going to cut her in two pieces and we know it is not real and it is simply a trick but nevertheless we are amazed by what we see because we don't know how it is done.
Sometimes I really wonder what all this maneuvering is all about when the solution is always the same. Change the debt to a new one. Is it to scare off the public servant of a country? Is it to create worries to the layman or just to rattle investors to that they make the wrong moves?
All these paper shuffling and meetings are a pie in the sky, smoke and mirrors and we believe it somehow.
Another finger to the layman.

JUNE 11-2011 BLOOMBERG NEWS.

After an almost 2% drop this week in the DJII and a six straight week lost, it begins to look like a correction. Hitting below the 1200 mark is not a good psychological barrier. Week economic performances are worrying investors but I think that the deficit talks are mudding hopes for the near future. I don't take the US deficit lightly but too much is said about it since Republicans are milking the story and belabouring the point.

It is going to get settled regardless since the government has the capacity to do so by raising taxes and still spending the 600 billion left in QE2.

It is too bad that Austin Goolsbee, the White House economist, is returning to Chicago University because he seems the only economist saying the real things, right to the point with no ''if'' and ''buts'' and ''maybes'' like Bernanke's ''dancing with the stars'' approach.

Greece find himself at a standstill as Trichet's ECB turns the table to the government for settling its problems. ECB won't participate in increasing its debt holding of Greek Bonds. Commodities were mixed all around, only Wheat increase by almost 2%.

JUNE 14, 2011-BLOOMBER NEWS

Presently we don't need good news from the U.S. to give a little rally on stocks. Good news from China suffices.

China said that Industrial production rose 13.2% and Product sale rose 16.9% in May.

Hey! Good enough for me.

Even if U.S. numbers are sluggish and OPEC doesn't seem to agree on the production quotas and Greece can't come up with the compromise it needs to fix his debt. The trio comprised of the ECB and IMF and the Greece government is at a standstill. According to Trichet, the people have to get behind the new bonds to bail out its government.

JUNE 16-2011-BLOOMBERG NEWS & CNN NEWS

When bad news is bad news and good news is bad news. The stock markets don't know where to go in regards to China's economic performance.

When a slowdown in economic activity is announced, the stock markets fall since China is a major trader with the US. When good news is announced about the industrial production increase and production sales, the stock markets fall since it means the price of oil is going to increase on China's increase in demand. It does cut both ways.

Even adding to the fire, the I.E.A org. forecast a long term increase of world consumption of 95.3 million barrels a day by 2016. Presently world consumption is pegged to be 88.0 million barrels a day.

Now, even the Eifel tower looks like an oil rig.

If you put the Greece political turmoil on top of its financial imbroglio, since he wants to shuffle ministers that don't agree with the austerity program, one is facing another major impasse.

Back in the US, things are not getting any better since Obama spoke of increasing the debt ceiling in order to prevent another financial crisis. The $14.3 trillion ceiling won't be enough and he is pleading Republicans and Democrats alike to pass this new bill in Congress.

Since the rest of the QE2 spending, the 600 billion has been deployed, analyst are waiting if QE3 is going to be announced. The methanol subsidy bill didn't pass Congress. It would have shaved $5 billion of the worst program ever invented.

ZCU11 - Corn (CBOT) - Daily OHLC Chart
Op:668-4, Hi:677-0, Lo:665-2, Cl:674-4

Agricultural commodities are seeing red in spite of the
internecine wars in the Middle East continues it ravage. The
world is focused on the national debt and confirmation of
economic performance to come.
The most important agricultural commodities futures like;
corn, wheat, CBT and KCB and soybean and soybean oil and
soybean meal and oats are lower than the beginning of the
month which we pegged on our monthly tab. (See page 241)
So far during the month of June, agricultural commodities are
reassuringly cheaper since the last two weeks.

The end of June is coming and investors and analysts are
trying to see trough the future the next governmental action as
the fog dissipates slowly. Is QE3 will be in effect or not?

In Canada, the worst news is that the Vancouver Canucks lost
the Stanley Cup to Boston.
There is always next year.

JUNE 17-2011-BLOOMBERG NEWS
CONTINUE THE REVOLUTION WITHOUT ME.

Middle East's unrest as played out as analyst focussed on Greece's management of its debt crisis and US growth. After shuffling the cabinet, Greece's president is finding conciliatory response in German leader willing to make some compromise.

As I said before, Greece debt has to get settled no matter what because there is no way out besides renegotiating the numbers and maturity. Even if the numbers are high, 19% on their 10 year bonds, they have time on their side; the future, since governments live for ever.

Since there is no devaluation possible since they don't have a specific currency, they are all in this together, Germany and the EU, ECB and the Euro.

These quiescent moments between negotiators give the US stock market some hope that things are going to be settled after all.

They were no question in my mind that resolution had to come and there was no point to overly react oscillating the stock market up and down of 1% every day besides giving speculators some room to manoeuvre. Remember that one can make money when the market goes down as well as up. Shorting the indices market or stocks or buying put options. Market's overreaction is voluntary in order to give traders something to do; making money.

While the people of the House Representative are busy showing their wieners on the net, other countries' leaders are showing real concern about real problems like the increase of food commodity prices by *speculators on the markets* as they rattle the world of their insecurities.

Minister Bruno Le Maire, a French minister is calling the G-20 countries to get real about food prices, food supply and food reserves so that countries get the real picture where the world stands. Taking for granted that population will increase to 9.2 billion people by the year 2050, it is now the time to play straight with food reserves so that steps can be taken.

Countries are too secretive about production and reserve of various foods to protect their market price as the world is worrying about quick price increase and what the future holds, creating riots all over the world.

''The G-20 countries have to be more transparent about food reserves and get serious about cooperating among themselves.'' Say Bruno Le Maire, guided by Sarkozy's seriousness on getting a hand on the food question based on the OECD's report that production is going down from 2.6% increase to 1.7% increase.

''Speculation only brings volatility in markets which disrupt production,'' he said.

The minister also criticized the US of using corn (13%) and sugar cane (30%) and vegetable oil (15%) to make additive for gasoline while food commodities are going rapidly upwards.

True that there is an obesity crisis in the US, so food is plentiful. Feeding the RAM is more important than one's feeding his family!

JUNE 21-2011-BLOOMBERG'S NEWS & CNN NEWS
BERNANKE'S SHOWDOWN AT THE OKAY CORAL

The stock market didn't know where to go these last few days as we approach the June 23 date of the long awaited move from Bernanke's high chair. Markets shrug off the Tunisian revolution and the rest of Arab's unrest for economic news at home. Even Greek's dilemma is beginning to lose its specter on markets as an agreement must be reached.

Even if OPEC members are coyly negotiating between themselves about production, it is taken with a grain of salt by markets back home while the ubiquitous presence of possible QE3 incentive will be unravelled very soon.

More importantly, so it seems, is the $2.2 trillion additional ceiling Obama is trying to get approval from Congress not to default on his debt. Vice president Bidden is trying to get a budget cut of $4.0 trillion to pass Congress with some difficulty from Republicans. It is a question of how real this cut is and where it is taken from.

Bernanke will address the public tomorrow but has markets are telling us today, by going up, that there won't be any more added stimulus and interest rates will stay where they are until further notice.

Bernanke's problem is the lagging economy with 9.0% unemployment which can't seem to get off the ground. Until then, it's *status quo.*

I can't understand why, and I am not alone, why Congress can't cut off the ethanol subsidies and the subsidies or getting back allowable write offs to major international oil companies for exploration? It is by getting back $ billions which would add up to $ trillions instead of cutting Medicare and Medicaid other social programs.

JUNE 22 -2011-BERNANKE'S ANNOUCEMENT THIS AFTERNOON-BLOOMBERG NEWS

This is where CNN stops influencing Bloomberg' news. Wars and riots and disingenuous political leaders stop influencing the stock market and oil market at home.

Only Greece's political shuffle paid off as the debt ridden country managed to postpone new package until July after the austerity plan is redrawn.

As I mentioned before concerning debt default of a country, there aren't much creditors can do besides rearranging the figures and the terms. Nobody is going to seize the Parthenon.

June 22- 2.15 pm.
DEAD AHEAD

Bernanke's announcement is neutral, to say the least. When in doubt, stay out, an old market saying when nobody known what to do. No moves is good news according the market and analyst alike. The rate will remain at 0.0% to .25% and the last of the QE2 600 $ billion purchase will go through as said and we will see, said Bernanke in the last comment since the economy can't shrug off this 9.1% unemployment. Figures shows wind age as the last GDP growth for the month of May was 1.8 % annualised from 3.1% the previous month.
Stocks have remained almost unmoved by the announcement to slightly negative territory and the Brent upward to 113.9 or 2.69% and the WTI up 1.06% to 95.170. Most of agricultural commodities are seeing red except for only a few.
Now markets, stocks and commodities don't know where to go. Waiting for some news to stimulate markets again so that profits can be made again?
Let's see; wars and riots: that has been done.
Sex scandals? Nobody cares anymore where politicians put their wieners.
Floods have been good but this is not the season.
How about another earthquake? Or a Tsunami?
We will see shortly on which market can get a hold on to make us pay.
As for me, I can see a summer doldrums ahead for market since there is no beacon to lead markets to be either optimistic or pessimistic.

JUNE 23-2011-BLOOMBERG NEWS

Obama's cut on military is an excellent sign of pulling back on wars, but for the next year, 1/3 of the troops back home will only cut cost by $100 billion. I'm happier of the potential lives saved by this gesture than the money saved.
The market's reaction of Bernanke's absolute bearing on the economy takes the DJI under 12,000 at 11,929 in early morning trading. The Jobless claims upward direction is more the cause of sliding stock markets. All commodity markets are in the red territory; energy and agriculture and even precious metals. Only NASDAQ is in the positive territory.
Greece's specter is still around thinking it might be hurtful to all European banking.
Greece is the weakest link in the EURO agreement and I don't think it could bring down all the other stronger, more industrialized countries like France, Italy and Germany.

PM fix-June 23-2011
It's really too bad that the International Energy Reserves will release from its Strategic Reserve 2 million barrels a day up to 30 days to alleviate Libya's *reduction just now*. Why? I'm utterly surprised about why *so late in the game*? Why not when Libya was at the forefront of the news? Why letting oil go up as much as 42% this year before using the reserves to calm pricing increase? Why wait until high prices choked the economy before reserves were used?
Isn't why reserves are there for, when there a potential reduction of supply coming?
When North American people were worried to death about gas prices, changing people's mind about further spending, THAT WAS THE TIME to bring in the Strategic Reserves and let the economy hum away peacefully.
Could be the reason why unemployment is stuck at 9.1%, jobless claims are up this week?

We have been belaboring Libya's case for months until it was no longer a problem, until people got in their mind that it wasn't such a big deal after all on total oil stock available. Wars and revolutions where politically exerted from our worries and we only had to concentrate on our economic performance to get the US economy going again. Unemployment-inflation and QE3 were our only concern. Now that oil is receding from its high price in May of $114.27 on the WTI, now the reserves are coming. It should have been done prior to May so that it would have alleviated the price increase.

The reserve ''cavalry'' comes in when the town as burned down. Too late!!

Where were you when we needed you?

Now we are going to wait until next month to see the unemployment figure or wait until the next quarter, or the one after that.

The Brent is down almost 6% today and the WTI is down to $91.070, 4.55%.

I think I'm going to take the summer off!!

JUNE 24-2011-BLOOMBERG NEWS

Markets are not reacting well after Bernanke's speech and the Strategic Reserve announcement of putting 30 million barrels of fine oil on the market.

The Down Jones, S&P are both down and the Brent oil index is down to $105.86 and the WTI is at $90.96

As I said yesterday, it was ''kinda'' late to dump oil on the market when prices were soaring in March, April and May. It is clear that both the President and Bernanke realized that high prices of oil or gasoline in the spring did affect the economy. Most analysts thought that the prices had to go much higher in order to be detrimental to the recovery. But guess what?

It was too high in the spring and now they just realized it.

The present availability is not because of the possible shortage since prices have been going down steadily for weeks now and everyone realized that Libya's production is not that much on worldwide production. Who said that Libya did stop production anyway?

Now these politicians are saying: Well, maybe paying close to $4.00 gallon was too high.

They didn't have their ears on the track, listening to the people complaining about the high prices which made them to differ expenses overall.

To reiterate the ''Oil market'' is the quantity not refined and sold to the retail outlet by major oil companies which are fully integrated, meaning that they exploit oil wells, they refine it into commercial gasoline and sold by their retail outlets. So far, there is no market for oil.

Since they produce more than what they can handle, they sell barrels of oil on the market which represent 40% of the production. This market is divided in many sub markets but being put to the highest bidder on the trading floor for countries to buy.

So, this is where the price increase occurs, 40% of the oil is being bid up and take the 60% remaining at the same level, and call it the ''international'' price.

As I mentioned before, that a Saudi Arabia minister said; if governments around the world are worried because of high oil prices, they should do something about it since they make more money out of a barrel of oil that we do. Since government tax on a percentage basis, they make more money when prices go up. If they only would have cut their taxes to reduce the retail price of gasoline, maybe it would have changed the unemployment figure today. Now, there are willing to make the price lower on oil by feeding the market of 2 million barrels a day and thus eventually gasoline (they say about .50 per gallon expected) so that the consumer can start spending elsewhere.

It is so appalling to see this non reaction when it was time and written on the wall so clearly.

JUNE 29-2011-BLOOMBERG NEWS.

All markets were up yesterday after oscillating for weeks waiting for Bernanke's decision on QE3 and the confirmation of the bank rate. The open market operation will be done sparingly as the U.S. economic vessel is panting along. Energy commodities were up 2.5% in the morning but slid down to +1.21% and all agricultural commodities and precious metals were up slightly.

Even if Greece hasn't solved its financial crisis, investors are optimistic that a compromise will be reached. Not exactly good timing for the Greek' Labour Union to demonstrate on the streets and go on strike since it creates another major imbroglio to be settled.

I did mention a few pages back the U.S. dollar might come back to the gold standard or have the world currency change not necessarily using the Yuan as China would like but something new for big trade purchases like oil. I have mentioned that the World Bank uses SDR, special drawing rights for its members which is a basket of currencies and it might extend its role to stabilize the fluctuations of the US dollar.

Nomura Securities are suggesting exactly that and even to form another basket of currencies like the Yen, the Suisse franc, the dollar and the Euro. Even presently, large purchases should be made by forming this basket in order to reduce currency fluctuations.

This is where the World Bank can intervene with its members to settle oil purchases using this basket or SDR. Since every country buys oil or sells oil, the World Bank should do the accounting and keeping the books.

GOOD NEWS AND BAD NEWS

The good news is that the IEA is putting oil on the market in order to reduce consumer spending on energy and bringing the price down. Now analysts say the cause of that might or may as it is literally written, make OPEC reduce production. So, prices moved upwardly.

Frankly, I'm sure no one knows what OPEC is going to do. This is why this coalition or cartel was created for to keep secret what they want to do. I don't think you would see Wall Street reporters at the meeting. I think that is just another reason to have higher prices and make room for traders to make money.

No wonder we don't have jobs in North America when HP Co. is expanding its research in China, said the California based computer company. Hewitt Packard has been in China since 1985 and has 20,000 employees. It would be nice if those jobs were here.

The banking industry can still smell the smoke coming from the 2008's egregious catastrophe
since lawyers are still burning midnight oil to solve the remainder of the dissonant cobweb.

Bank of America agreed to pay $8.5 billion in a settlement of the defunct bonds relating to AGO assured mortgages by Fannie May and Freddie Mac. (I don't know who came up with those names for mortgage companies; they sound more like a Waffle & Pancake and Burger joints.) Anyway......

Most are getting about .20 on the dollar. But BA's problems are not over yet since the MBI, the bond insurer, is suing for $21 billion Countrywide, BA's mortgage company for being in default on 91% of its application forms which discrepancies

were made stating false income by mortgage applicants, wrong credit score or a wrong debt / income ratio.
Lehman Brothers is still grinding the stone with a liquidation plan of $65 billion for bond holders. Goldman Sachs Group and Morgan Stanley are some of the holders.
The web we weave!!

FIRST OF JULY-BLOOMBERG NEWS

The stock markets are up third day in a row based on the Greece budget crisis will go through and U.S manufacturing news is good. The DJ crossed the 12,500 mark as the S&P follows.
The Brent is at 110.85 and WTI at 94.55 and Gold and Silver are weak.
Some analysts and investors like George Soros and economists like Niall Fergusson from Harvard are genuinely concerned by Greece's not being able to finance itself (debt 150% of GDP) even when temporary austerity measures are taken but on the same day, it seemed that the public will finance $124 billion and the rest from the IMF and European banks. The problem seemed to have been solved.
Its trading partners are Germany and Italy and China and most exports are food and beverages, manufacturing, petrol products, chemicals and textile.
The main industry is tourism and shipping and unemployment is at 16%.
JULY 4TH 2011
Today, it is Canada day and the mostly popular newly weed couple is here. Stock markets have performed well during the week, up over 5%, so it is time to take some time off.

JULY FIFTH-2011-BLOOMBERG NEWS
This is the time to do our monthly check on commodities. See: Appendix Price Monthly Movement on page 241.

The major indexes are Brent crude Oil at $114.39 the same as March -04-2011 and the WTI is at $941.250, below March and above February.

These commodities were a major concern for all of us particularly on the retail prices of gasoline. Today, retail prices posted on June 27 are; $3.574 gallon from almost $4.00 and 130.4 cents a litre from 146.9 cents in Canada.

It is quite a relief from its high and most people stopped bitching about it.

We tried to highlight the moving factors by following the events of the good and the bad news published daily and tried to see the real reasons for hikes and fall of the precious liquid. Without reiterating all I've said, you can surely revised day by day the world events, and I'm glad to see that we were not running out of oil at today's prices indicate. It is not the supply of the Strategic Oil reserve either and it is not the tightening up of OPEC's supply either.

We came close of producing what we consume (worldly) and with the havoc of wars, disturbance on all Middle East countries created an opportunity for traders in the Future's market to increase prices. We saw that there was no physical shortage even if Libya stopped totally its production.

Economic news from the US, if we were getting out of recession or if the recovery was too slow affected daily prices. European news of National banks being in default and of course, the US deficit made headlines almost every day. Frankly, is anything changed from what has been since the beginning of the year?

Fundamentally, no.

Did prices fluctuate to levels of worrying everyone on the planet?

Unfortunately, yes.

The news that made those fluctuations erratic and presently the world seemed to be humming along on getting stronger. In the last twelve months, commodities varied from 20% to 95%

(Source: IndexMondi.com) and some more just on was published in newspapers. No one but speculators wants to see prices of raw staple going up. No one wants to spend more on food than what they we have too. The Commodity Price Index has risen of 32% since the middle of 2010 to February 2011, (Source: IMF). Sure we had bad crops and increase demand from Emerging markets and false demand was created on possible scarcity of grains and other foods. We did have to pick in our supply or (stock) but was it warranted the 32% increase? Today, the IMF says we should recover quickly our supply of stock.

We were lead to believe more that we were running out of food or runaway inflation to the point where one have to start his own garden or just die. Today, *corn* and *wheat* and *soybeans* have decreased considerably.

119

Fertilizers were up more than the underlying commodities they are used for. Cattle Feeder Future was up constantly and still at all-time high. Some chemical companies did make a lot of profits in those times. I can't wait to check their yearend profits.

I think I can sum up all these fluctuations on ''newspaper fluff'' using a nicer term than the one I have in mind. You have good news daily and bad news daily and you have conflicting news and you have news that creates opposite reactions. Example: Good economic news will push prices of oil on the market, meaning that demand will increase. Take your pick.

The rest of the year will confirm this as we get behind of this so called ''recovery.''

The only thing about market's reactions to all this, is at some point, the stocks markets become high, or over purchased and a sell off will occur, being profit taking. And perhaps stocks will become cheaper according to some and reasonable to others and promising in the future creating a buying opportunity until they become overly expensive based on the historical performances, not the real worth. If things are flying again, it will be curtailed by fraud and embezzlements and we will go another round of the same old thing, making traders richer or poorer.

JULY 7-2011 BLOOMBERG NEWS. –THE GOOD, THE BAD AND THE UGLY.

As I mentioned yesterday, that markets reacts to good news or bad news and when good news is bad and bad news is even worst or good news for some.

The good news is that jobless claim in the US is down, manufacturing output is up in the UK and interest rates are up in China and going up in Europe to curb inflation. So oil futures are going up. Brent is up over 3% and the WTI is up 2.3%

The stock market has more optimism investors than pessimism investors since it is up early morning to 88 points but the big ''ticket item'' coming up soon on August 2 is the debt payment of the US government which is short of cash by 44% of its revenues.

The interest on Chinese bonds or American solders' pay or Iowa farmers or Social Security recipients might forgo their payments until Obama gets approval of increasing the debt ceiling to $14.3 trillion.

It is getting to be a close call since politicians are now commenting on how ''grave'' this would be for the world and the US and its rating, if any default would occur.

''Impossible'' some say, to even think about it.

The government has a choice of raising taxes, put its hand in the cookie jar at Fort Knox and sell some gold, which the Chinese will be glad to buy instead of US securities from the Treasury or due both in a milder manner to ease the investor's insecurities or prevent the US dollar to take a major fall.

There is not too many things left on the table and a hand full of players and the stakes are enormously high. This is what I call a real ''poker game.''

One good news is that the regulators are beginning to realize that the white collar crooks, the one that are sipping 85 year old Porto and smoking Cuban cigars (which is illegal to import by the way) at tax payer's expense, *the bank's financial executives* are made responsible if their banks were liquidated by using the ''Claw Back'' law to have these executives pay back from their own salary and bonuses for money lost, said the Deposit Insurance Corp.

Like I said previously, it is a *personal decision* from executives whenever they make a move for ''the bank'' and should be *personally held responsible* for their actions. Hiding under the corporate charter or chapter 11 is no more allowed. No more guile from the Hampton's mansion.

Another good news is that the financial companies involved in illegal repossessing of houses are still fighting like rats in a can full of water against each other. BA and JPM and MNL Corp, Hermitage, Kremlin and All State Co. are chewing each other tails in billions of dollar lawsuits. Their contentious departments are keeping busy, very busy.

JULY 8TH. 2011 –BLOOMBERG NEWS.

My evaluation of good news and bad news yesterday was indeed timely because today, it's not only the good and the bad mixed together it is the ugly; US payroll added 18,000 jobs and the Jobless claims rose to 9.2%. This is the same coin where the other side is supposed to be opposite from each other. I think the compilation of statistics should be revised.

One thing for sure which was mentioned long time ago when we were in the eye of the financial crisis and now being confirmed by Warren Buffet is, the jobless rate will only come down if the housing market gets back to health. In other words, the cause of it all will have to be the cure. Today, they are still too many houses on the secondary market at cheap prices thus handicapping the construction industry for new housing which would create jobs for carpenters, plumbers, electricians and all other subcontractors and suppliers presently out of work.
Construction is the first sign of growth followed by durable good sales, house whole products and automobile sales.

JULY 12-2011-BLOOMBERG NEWS

Armageddon continues for President Obama and the
Republicans on the approval of increasing the deficit to 14.3
trillion to cover payments due on bonds and other obligations
on **August the second**.
Since things are not easy to settle between the two parties
which are clearly going for a chicken race until **August
second**, the markets are worried. The Dow was down 150
points, showing investors are not convinced that there is a fix
for this financial impasse. On top of this, Europe is seeing the
cloud of Greece's imbroglio spreading through Europe,
covering Italy in its shadow.

The only good news is that the S&P GSCI Agricultural Index
shows relief as concern of food shortage is easing. There is a
doubling of short sales on the Index on wheat. All agricultural
commodities were down yesterday and the WTI below $95
and the Brent at $117.

POLITICAL WRENCH

Where was the political ''wrench'' in the mist of the recession
to start saving money on big tickets spending by Government
in order to save the day; the **August second** is the day of
reckoning.
I admit that it's easy to say after the fact ; You should have
done this and that……. but let us remind yourself that
Governments have to see a few years ahead in order to balance
the books.
-I would have freeze the space shuttle program which will be
done after the last flight.
-I would have cut the subsidies on corn transformation to
ethanol.

-I would have cut the oil exploration subsidies (or tax refund) of big oil companies
 for their exploration programs.
-I would have fixed the loophole of American companies transferring their head office into tax free or tax reduced countries and not paying US taxes.
-I would have revised the personal income tax for billionaires and millionaires which don't pay taxes way before today. A minimum tax would have been feasible.
-Cut military expenses by getting out gradually out of Afghanistan and Iraq.

These moves are politically popular to execute but the fact remained that they were doable. Cut military expenses would have been difficult but it is going to be done eventually but now it seems to be too late.
I don't really know who much all these savings represent if these programs were cut or eliminated but surely the *August the second day of dead reckoning*   would not be a concern.
Unfortunately, there is a lot of national pride that would have been blemished if the US government would have openly admitted that they can't afford to go to war anymore.
Better to swallow our pride and save some lives than facing bankruptcy. Remember the Soviet Union which was forced to fold because they couldn't afford going to war anymore.
It was a war of financial attrition. If you take all these saving put together and invest in infrastructure, I would have created jobs and the 9.2% unemployment would have been reduced by quite a lot.
University professor Laura Taylor from UCLA mentioned that 30,000 jobs can be created by spending $1 billion on infrastructure. The other point she is making is during the last decade no major expenses were allocated in infrastructure, thus giving lots of room to execute those tangible investments.

Too much money has been going into financial markets and the communication industry.

I'm not saying that Google and Yahoo and RIM and Apple don't create jobs but I would be surprised to see how much the (employee /sales ratio) of those companies as opposed to manufacturing.

JULY 14-2011-BLOOMBERG NEWS

Captain America spoke. Bernanke said yesterday that he will put Q3 on the table and markets reacted.

The dollar went down and gold & silver went up. The good news is that the US trading partner, China has an annual growth rate of 9.7% for the first quarter and 9.5% for the second quarter. When markets goes up when someone else economy is going well, there is sensitivity there.

And Japan had the industrial production increase substantially. So, the stock market went flying early yesterday to 150 points (DJ) higher to finish at plus 44 points. The oil markets followed by an increase in the Brent and WTI fears that inflation will come soon and prices are going to be much more expensive. Commodities attracted more money as other investment lags.

No talks about rates or inflation, but as gold went up substantially it means the investors are thinking about it and at the real purchasing power as the USD goes down.

Funny enough that most countries like China and ECB are increasing their interest rates since inflation is showing its ugly head in those countries. The IMF published rates of inflation for the last month for June 2011 (annualised): Canada 3.7%

US at 3.6%

India at 8.7%

Brazil at 6.6%

Russia at 9.6%

South Africa at 4.6%

China at 4.6%

The IMF Index for Fuel and non-fuel Price Index at 100 in 2005.
2006 at 120.71
2007 at 134.97
2008 at 172.13
2009 at 118.80
2010 at 142.48
2011 at 144.21
It is easy to calculate since 2005,   prices are up 44% since then. Since the recession, at the trough of 2009, there has been an increase of 26%.
If Mr. Bernanke would come up and say exactly what the inflation rate is, he would feel obligated to raise rates and he is afraid it will take away the possibility of reducing the unemployment rate of 9.2%
Raising rates wouldn't be such a bad thing since it would support the USD and give real rates of return to bond holders. Now for a ten year bond, one gets a taxable 3% which mean almost nothing. At those anemic returns, money goes into the stock market and commodities pushing high prices.
At least if rate were up, the debt would be more easily financed internally.
The CD How Institute in Canada suggested that the Bank of Canada raises their internal bank rate to 1.25% taking effect on July 19. Usually, Canada and the US do act in tandem as far as rates are concerned.

European economies are not out of the woods yet since Italy is now under the dark cloud of debt financing, the same as Greece.

The August the second deadline for approval of raising the ceiling of the national debt is like the O.K Coral standout with

Democrats and Republicans. Republicans don't want to raise taxes and Democrats don't seem to have a choice.

I don't think there is any choice since it is an obligation to pay the interest due on bonds which is money already borrowed. The question arises; will the Government forgo payment and face downgrading its rating?

Will the Government forgo payment on Medicare Medicaid and Social Security payments?

Or simply raise taxes?

Raising personal taxes wouldn't be so bad after all since the US personal income tax is relatively low.

One has to pay the piper eventually.

I don't think the American people would object of raising personal taxes. It seems logical and a small percentage from each contributor is less harmful to the economy than the other two alternatives.

Today's market negative reaction is due to the digestion of the news. Is Q3 on the table and waiting to see in the future is good or bad for the prospect of a recovering economy?

Some say yes and some say no. Stimulus comes with a cost: possible rapid inflation.

Is Moody's warning on degrading US bonds from AAA to whatever scarring the markets?

Ireland got degraded making it more expensive to raise debt. If that is the only drawback, it might happen.

The IEA mentioned that long term demand for oil is going to reach 90 MBD in the near future. We are not out of the woods yet depending on Saudi Arabia and other exporting countries for the precious light oil. Windmills are not producing enough per investment and space taken. Sun energy seems again too expensive to be widely commercial. What is left and is still cheap is natural gas and that there is plenty of it.

Trucks and taxis should be converted into natural gas as soon as possible since the price of oil will continue to rise with increasing demand.

Many countries are not as sluggish as the US. Looking at India and Brazil, which are really flying and also emerging countries which are in fact: emerging?

Let's look at coffee to see if there is going to be a surge since it is mentioned that Colombia experienced a ravage on crops by a storm which affected 40% of crops.

All agricultural commodities are down today, seeing red, losing yesterday's increase, including coffee and the Brent and the WTI. Only gold and silver remained on the green side.

JULY 16-2011-BLOOMBERG NEWS

The market closed slightly positive yesterday wondering if Q3 is going to be good or bad and create runaway inflation. If the markets thought it was a good thing, gold and silver wouldn't have gone up. Confidence in the dollar would have manifested, which clearly didn't.

The vague statement of Bernanke about inflation is depressing since BLS mentioned that all Items are at 3.6% increase. Bernanke is fixated on saying that he wants core inflation rate should be between 1.5 to 2.0 %.

Since the BLS mentioned 20 items which includes food and oil, I have added all 20 items on a percentage and divided by 20 (I am a math wizard) and come up with 8.2% inflation on the average for all items. With gas and food of 30% increase, one can't come up with only 3.6%.

Since most people spend at least 50% of their disposable income on food and gas, this represents a big chuck if their income. 30% /.50= 15%

Markets are not going anywhere until August the second to see if the US bond system is going to be downgraded. And then......

JULY 18-2011-BLOOMBERG NEWS

When I said that markets were not going anywhere until August second deadline, I meant that they wouldn't go anywhere but south. Markets in early trading today are losing 1% on the Dow and the S&P and all commodities are down, even energy commodities except precious metals which have crossed the barriers of $1600.oz for gold and $40.oz for silver. Markets are now probably realizing that, even if the ceiling of debt is raised, it only mean kicking the can down the road and it will be more expensive if Standard & Poor's downgrade US Bonds. The problem wouldn't be solved in the long run. Republicans are looking at 1 out of 3 dollars coming in for the budget cuts and raising taxes as it did in the 80's in the Regan years when a similar problem was faced. Then, a compromise can be reached by allowing some increase in the deficit ceiling.

The USD is taking a beating since one has to sell dollars to buy gold.

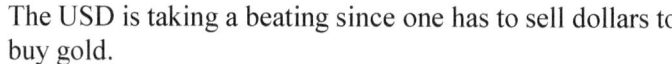

JULY 19-2011. BLOOMBERG NEWS

Good economic data makes markets fly early morning. Some big corporations are showing good earnings like IBM and Coca Cola but more importantly, housing starts are improving quite nicely and office rental in California is up considerably from low 2010.

These are good signs when real estate is picking up. As I said before, the recovery will show signs in the sector that suffered the most. This is the antidote the economy needs, which is investment where the yoke of the problem was at the beginning.

Another good news in Canada, where Melanie Atkins antitrust regulator for the Bureau of Competition is acting like ''Wonder Woman'' confronting big corps on their illegal practices.

She took to court Visa and Master Car for overly charging merchants. Bell Canada for misleading ads of its pricing and Air Canada and the Canadian Real Estate Association and the Real Estate Board. Now she is looking at the sale of the TSE by a consortium of banks and funds.
She is not asleep at the helm and not afraid to put the hammer down to nail the big corporation culprits. Way to go Melanie!

At market close, some good news waiting came as the President agreed to a bipartisan deficit cutting of $3.7 trillion and a tax increase and raising of the ceiling of the deficit, a mixed bag of everything to bring things back on track.
Dow Jones up 200 points for a 1.62%
S&P up 20 points for 1.59%
NASDAQ 59 points for 2.14%
Confidence in the dollar was visible against the YEN and the Suisse Franc as gold and silver retreats. Agricultural and Energy Commodities were mostly upward.
Now the biggest hurdle is out of the way. Would this mean a summer rally?
Everything is blue sky now.

JULY 21-2011-BLOOMBERG NEWS

The optimists surpassed the pessimisms on early trading today as Obama is dotting the i's and crossing the t's on the partisan agreement. The EU is getting close to solve the debt crisis of its own and corporate profits is showing good numbers and manufacturing activity is improving in the mitts of an increase in jobless claims which increased by 10,000.
We are getting closer to August 2 but it seems like things are going to get fixed by then.

JULY 23-2011-BLOOMBERG NEWS-TANGLED IN A TANGO

As close as things were getting to reach an agreement between Republicans and Democrats, both are out of step as John Boehner walks away from the dance floor.
The debt ceiling augmentation seemed to have been reached but the increase in the tax component is breaking the dance between both parties.
The same type of scenario is going on in Europe as a deal seemed to have been reached to finance Greece with public borrowing for 70% of its debt load, now EU officials are considering allowing Greece to go into default as other countries are in line like Spain and Italy to be bailed out.

Markets have nowhere to go but down as we approach the August second deadline to solve these two debt overhangs on both sides of the Atlantic.

If countries default on their debt it only means that lower rating will be initiated and the cost of borrowing will be higher than before. Of course debt holders will be left holding the bag without their interest payments. Will that be so bad? I really wonder.
It would be bad for the markets but for us, us which are in the real economy, will it make a difference? Yes, if the army pay checks are held back and pensioners are not receiving their money but I don't think this is going to happen. Interest on foreign held bonds will come first, not Medicare and Medicaid or other contingency payments.
What happens if interest is not paid on U.S. Bonds? It could only be postponed to a future time. Many corporations (and the big ones) did encompass such a dilemma when the kittle was dry.

Chrysler, GM and the others were in this conundrum before and there are not dead yet.

This debt problem can't go on forever. It has to be settled and settle soon and I believe it will. It is a matter of reorganizing the numbers; rates, terms and the amount, (rolling it over, using a banking term) and life will go on. Is it a fear tactic by some? We shall see in the next few weeks.

JULY 25-2011-BLOOMBERG NEWS--STALEMATE WEEKEND

The weekend negotiations were hard as both parties, Democrats and Republicans find themselves in a stalemate position when the Armageddon week ends on August second. Markets went flying south early morning trading on the futures market as gold reaches an all- time high. The Swiss Franc did follow gold against the greenback and other currency as Greek's rating has been downgraded by Moody's, cutting rating to Ca from Caa1. Standard & Poor's remains CCC. Wall Street backs Republican House speaker John Boehner as party contributions totaled $6.6 million for his campaign committee, six times more than the Ohio Republican received during the same period two years ago when he was the chamber's minority leader.

Who said the dollar was losing power?

Employees at the New York hedge fund Paulson & Co. contributed $61,050 to Boehner's campaign account, more than any other campaigns. New York based Moore Capital Management LLP employees gave $53,000, while at Cantor Fitzgerald LP donated $45,000.

Republican consultant Eddie Mahe said that he had no doubt Wall Street has been betting that the House Republican majority would lead the effort to ''repeal or at least modify'' the revised financial regulations enacted last year.

Boehner and House Republicans last year opposed passage of the revamped rules for the financial industry, which was blamed for triggering the worst economic downturn since the Great Depression.

President Obama signed those new rules into law a year ago this month. Since taking control of the House, the Republican majority has moved to ''undo'' parts of the legislation despite the Democrats Senate has prevented major changes.

The Commodity Futures Trading Commission, which is writing most of the new derivatives rules, and the House Appropriation Committee voted to limit funding for the new consumer protection bureau.

House Republicans have also opposed Democratic efforts to tax carried interest, the share of profits as part of legislation paid to asset managers, as ordinary ''income'' rather than at lower ''capital gains'' rate.

The Managed Fund Association spent $2 million in the first six months of this year lobbying Congress on Financial regulations and other issue, according to its lobbying disclosure.

The purchasing power of American consumers has been eroded when buying imported cheese and French wine but here at home, the dollar is still strong when buying power.
If money can't buy happiness, it can buy just about everything else.

JULY 27-2011-MY OWN PREDICTIONS

As the world waits for the August second deadline, the filibusters are still in a gridlock over the debt ceiling approval. Most people don't know what is going to happen if the Standard & Poor's downgrades the US sovereign bonds and if the ceiling is going to be approved.
I will be bold with my predictions;

First, I think there is too much *pride* in this insecure behavior from the US is the biggest economy in the world and most international trades are done in USD. The dollar is sinking ever since the concern and still sinking and that is *the* devaluation of the US. Nothing really worst can happen (besides government devaluation) since markets have already done so against other currencies. In other words, the devaluation of the dollar has been done and will continue on the "currency markets."

Second, I think there is too much reliance over the rating since Standard & Poor is a private rating institution which has been wrong before. You remember the triple A rating of Lehman Brothers just before it collapsed? It's *just an opinion* and that won't sink the economy down the drain. The cost of the downgrading will increase the borrowing cost of maybe half a point but it represents something that can be handled. That will trigger an increase in all interest rate holdings but it will be better in the short and the long run since Treasury Bonds have a negative income.

The foreign market and the domestic market will decide what return it should be on government securities. Remember that US Government debt is comprised of $4.5 trillion foreign and $ 9.8 trillion domestic. I think the citizens will create the "just return" on its own government debt in the market.

The downgrading will happen just the same if ceiling is increased since it is not the debt increase that is at play, it is the cuts of government spending and how much income can be increase down the road and how it will all end up in the next year or two, in other words, if it is reasonable and possible to envisage a balanced budget in the next five years or ten years. That is what is at stake, not the ceiling of the debt.

In summary, a compromise will be reached and ceiling will be approved and the rating will be downgraded and life will continue as *all Governments* struggle around the world to get out of this financial conundrum. There is more pride involved than the actual consequences.

The most likely to lose are the US banks which are holding government Treasuries in large quantity. If they lose a half point in yield, that represent a large sum of money.

Let us keep in mind it was the American banks and other lending institutions which put the Government in this bind by irresponsible risk taking in the first place.

The trillions given last year for the bailout would be welcome by now.

JULY 29-2011- VACATION TIME MEANS HIGHER GAS PRICE

It is inevitable, when vacation time comes, gas prices then to rise dramatically. In the Montreal area, gas prices rose by 10 cents per liter overnight making consumer annoyed. It was the beginning of this book, complaining about higher gas price during the x-mas holidays and now, it's the summer holidays. In this weak economy, I'm surprised that there isn't more political will to stop big oil companies to gouging the consumer so bluntly, almost at gunpoint (in this case with the nuzzle gun).

The official gas price is as of July 20, 139.9 cents per liter. (Gasticker.com)

In the US, no substantial price has shown yet since the official price is $3.699 per gallon on July 25. (EIA)

I'm sure though that, prices will increase close to $4.00 gal. soon.

AUGUST SECOND 2011 BLOOMBERG NEWS

Right down to the wire, as Republicans and Democrats agreed to settle the debt limit and agreed to spending cuts without increasing personal taxes. It was agreed last night and voted by

Congress and now awaiting for the Senate approval and then to the President to sign as a Bill. The numbers are pretty much in line of what Obama asked for but the Republicans stayed holding their guns foregoing the tax increase. In these negotiations, the Democrats have lost some feathers and the Republicans gained a few.

Today is probably one of the most important days in American history.

It has never been seen before where a Government bill took so much of the limelight around the world and so much was at stake.

Raising the ceiling of $2.1 Trillion and a budget cut of $2.4 without additional revenue is taking a chance of slowing employment by creating government layoffs rather than increasing taxes and be able to manage the deficit better and hoping to reduce the sovereign debt.

The stock markets are down not due to the deal, I think, but economic weakening in the automotive sector. Dow Jones is down 1.41%

S&P down 1.77%

NASDAQ down 1.81%

Brent crude F. at $116.66

WTI F. at $93.89

A non-related story is that *corn* inventories are low pushing the price of corn of 4.47% as well as *wheat* (CBT) in 5.4% and *oats* of almost 2.0%

SYRIA'S TURMOIL

With all eyes gawking on the US political spar between Obama and John Boehner, Syria's problems are not less significant in the eyes of the world since the death number has been accumulated close to 2,000 since March.

The population wants Bashar al Assad (son of Hatez al Assad) out of power and reforms of the Regime since the Emergency Law exists since 1963 suspending all constitutional protections.

The country' 22 million people mostly Muslims, are against the dictatorship of its so called Socialist leader. Hama, one of the biggest cities next to Damascus is the theater of the killings by the government's army on civilians.

Mainly an agricultural economy with some crude oil export of less than 200,000bl/day in 2005 has natural gas which is widely used by its residents.

Fighting wars is not new for Syrians since they fought the Arab-Israeli war in 1948 and the Yom Kippur war in 1973 which brought backers like the Soviet Union and the United States closer in confrontation and multitude of conflicts and overthrow governments is embedded deep in its long history as far back of thousands of years BC. Close to the Soviet Union since a pact was signed in 1956, its single party government resembles more of a despotic regime than a socialist government.

Its situation is probably going to turn similar to Libya since it is a replica of the same situation as the rest of the political world is getting involved by asking to stop the massacre on its people.

AUGUST 3-2011-BLOOMBERG NEWS

The battle has been won but the war is not over yet.

Most investors and people in general are happy that a new ceiling on the national debt has been raised but the fact remains that the governmental cuts are going to hurt the economy.

With poor figures of the performance of the economy which is still showing no real growth, markets are showing signs of pessimism as the market is still in the red zone.

The downgrading from the S&P and Moody's can still happens and will affect banks which are the biggest holders of Treasury Bonds.

Most agricultural commodities are down since demand might be reduced by a weak economy so as crude oil. Only gold and silver are up.

Let's look at our commodity Index during the beginning of the year to date, 7 months reckoning.

APPENDIX OF COMMODITY PRICES-MONTHLY MOVEMENTS

From Feb.04 to August 3 Change in %

ENERGY

Brent Crude Future (USd/bbl.)   100.180 to 113.87 a
13% increase.

Gas Oil Future (ICE)(USd/MT)   848.750 to 955.75 a
12.6% increase

Heating Oil Future(USd/gal.)   272.03 to 304.210 a
11.7% increase

Natural Gas Future(USD/MMBtu)   4.318 to 4.093 a
0.225% decrease

Gasoline RBOB Future USd/gal.)   244.60 to 295.66 a
20% increase

WTI Crude Future(USD/bbl.)   89.50 to 92.28   a
3% increase

AGRICULTURAL

Canola Future (WCE) (CAD3MT)   607.70 to 567.0   a
6 % decrease

Cocoa Future-LI(GBP/MT)   2,150.00 to 1,842.00 a
14.3% decrease

Cocoa Future(USd/MT)	3,282.0 to 2,921.0	a
11% decrease		
Coffee ''C'' Future(USd/lb.)	249.45 to 242.50	a
2.8% decrease		
Corn Future(USd/Bu	666.270 to 708.50	a
6.3% increase		
Cotton no.2 Future (USd/lb.)	168.270 to 105.100	a
37% decrease		
FCOJ-A-Future(USd/lb.)	172.600 to 199.85	a
16.8% increase		
Wheat Future (CBT)USd/Bu)	853.750 to 746.75	a
12.5% decrease		
Wheat Future (KCB) (USd/Bu)	943.00 to 793.25	a
16% decrease		
Sugar #11 (world) (USd/lb.)	32.840 to 27.88	a
15% decrease		
Soybean Future(USd/Bu)	1,431.0 to 1370.50	a
4.1 % decrease		
Lumber Future ($/1,000 board ft.)	300.90 to 223.40	a
25.6% decrease		
Oat Future(USD/Bu)	414.45 to 356.25	a
14% decrease		
Rough Rice (CBOT) (USDcwt.)	16.185 to 16.285	a
.01% increase		
Soybean-meal. Future (USd/lb.)	383.20 to 360.20	a
6.0% decrease		
Soybean Oil Future(USD/lb.)	58.98 to 57.48	a
2.5% decrease		
Wool Future (SFE)(cents/kg.)	1,175.0 to 1,376.0	a
17.2 % increase		
INDUSTRIAL METALS		
Copper Future(USd/lb.)	460.400 to 433.50	a
5.8% decrease		
PRECIOUS METALS		

Gold 100 oz. Future(USd/t.oz.)	**1,348.80 to 1670.80 a**
23.8% increase	
Silver Future (USd/t.oz.)	**28.93 to 41.675 a**
43.7% increase	
LIVESTOCK	
Live Cattle Future(USd/lb.)	**112.925 to 117.525 a**
3.9% increase	
Cattle Feeder Future(USd/lb.)	**125.100 to 135.00 a**
8.0% increase	
Lean Hogs Future(USd/lb.)	**91.30 to 91.250**
same.	

 Source: Bloomberg-Commodity Futures Online.

Commodities have peaked this year (see graph) but not up to this point since there are **15 commodities** that have *lost* ground since inception, in February 04-2011 to this point, August 03, 2011. They are **13 commodities** that have *gained* and one remaining stable out of 29 on the board.

All Energy commodities have peaked during the month of **May,** 8 agricultural commodities have peaked during the month of **February,** 4 in **March,** 3 in **April** and livestock in **April** as well. Some are at their peak today like Gold and Rough Rice Future (CBOT).

(See monthly report on page 241)

Gold increase is pretty much explanatory since the US dollar has plunged and so did the EURO because of possible EU banks failures and Governments unsolvable debts.

-**The month of May** was at the eye of Libya's war
-Gasoline was at their peak in North America
-Oil Companies declared a substantial increase in profits
-Bernanke is losing credit saying that inflated oil prices are transitory
-Investors and analyst wondered about Q3
-In Europe, Greek's crisis can't seem to reach a compromise
It was a month of full political news.

In February energy kept going upward but agricultural commodities as well since Egypt was trying to tame down its population demonstrating against high food prices. Demonstrations spread in all the Middle East countries as people were fed up of being subjected to their present ruling and high prices. Coffee and sugar and Oats went flying. Libya got into the picture during the month creating an additional chaotic situation.

Mayhem was spread in 12 countries resembling the end of civilization.

March and **April** were much of the same except that US warships were getting closer to Libya.

Energy prices increased since all the Middle East was in chaos. Russia announced that drought was responsible for cancelling their grain export and Saudi Arabia was getting involved militarily by sending troops to help Egypt.

Beside the rampant wars in the Middle East, some tornados and floods were inflicting the US, bringing more worries to the future prices of commodities.

My 7 month conclusion is that, news about oil and commodities are amplified by commodities traders which use the bad news to create volatility. Movements is self-propelled by more trades. It is a spiral which is created by traders making more profits.

Not that the bad news isn't real, like floods and droughts and the possible shortage of oil, but these news are ''milked'' to make a profit. When the news is released, it is only a possibility that it would affect crops and nobody knows how much, but the commodity in question goes flying on the CBOT. Today, no one is thinking about the shortage of food or the shortage of oil or the price of coffee or sugar since prices have fallen. It does prove my point, that only hype is involved and traders have had a very good year so far since 15 out of 29 commodities are trading lower than their price at the beginning of the year.

AUGUST 4 2011-BLOOMBERG NEWS
Just as I was about to write that markets didn't react much about the National Debt ceiling, only on some poor economic data, that today, all markets fell out of bed by hopping 4.31% for the DJIA and 4.78% for the S& P and 5.08% for NASDAQ and the TSE has fallen drastically as well and the Canadian dollar loss 4 basis points.
Yields on US Bonds have dropped significantly and all commodities are in the red territory.
The Brent as well as the WTI almost fell as much as stock markets. The job creation was 82,000 last month and jobless claims were 400,000 created fear that the US might be looking at a double dip recession.
These poor numbers certifies that QE 3 is in the offing. It does confirm that the US is not out of the woods while Switzerland and Japan are cutting their rates to liquefy their economy. The Euro was a concern as well since Italy and Spain are hoping for a bailout by the ECB.
I was thinking for a brief moment, one day that the corner was turned and we would slowly return to more normal times. I remembered writing that we would experience a summer doldrums and the last third and fourth quarter would experience a bull market.
Marc Fabber which I quoted many times did say the US stock markets would experience a 20% setback soon. So far, almost a 5% drop in one day is leading right in his predictions.

AUGUST FIFTH-2011-BLOOMBERG NEWS
Marylyn Monroe didn't sing ''Happy Birthday'' to Obama's 50th birthday, instead, he got a 500 point loss on the stock market as a present.

Still today, markets are down not happy with the economic numbers coming out and thinking that this is getting serious since now there is a chance of another recession coming our way.

Sometimes there are numbers which affect the perception of the economy and sometimes you have real factors like a margin call on stock holders since the markets have been going down for 8 days in a row.

Numbers are relative which I said before but on market reactions, they are usually based on predictions. Whatever numbers which are published, they either fall short of predictions made by analysts and economists and markets reacts downwards. Another thing reading news reports evaluating numbers, one sees a lot of; *'might, may, or could''* when forecasting the economy and I'm afraid that is enough to influence markets down or up, whatever the case may be. Markets are jittery this way, reacting on a daily basis without fundamentals.

Mr. Nouriel Roubini whose' reputation is no longer in question; see more than a 50% chance of another recession in the US. Annual growth might end up at 2% for this year which isn't enough to reduce unemployment to reasonable levels.

US markets are still down bringing all markets down with them; Australia, Canada, Asian as well as Taiwan, Singapore and the rest.

Since markets doubled since March 2009 without really experiencing economic growth, it became oversold by a long shot.

At the end of the day, US markets are in the green area but Europe and Asia and Canada are still losing big time.

Energy commodities are in the green area and agricultural commodities are mixed between green and red.

Retail gas is $ 3.71 gal. in the US and $1.39.9 litre in Canada. There is a price un-elasticity in regards to crude oil, meaning when the price of crude oil lowers, the price of retail remains the same. But the contrary when crude goes up, retail prices go up as well.

AUGUST 8 -2011 – STANDARD & POORS DOWNGRADES U.S RATING

The long awaited action by the rating company came through last Friday night, from the AAA rating to AA+. Now the question arises; will this sank treasuries and US bonds?
After a dismal week for equities around the world, (3% down yesterday all over) thinking that the US economy is not picking enough steam and the probability of seeing another recession this year came to the forefront of news influencing investors around the world to seek other investments. Other currencies have shown some strength like the Swiss Franc, the Australian dollar, the Canadian dollar, the New Zealand Kiwi and the Norwegian Crone.
Even if the ECB plowed money into Spanish bonds and some Italian bonds, the rest of the world are still confident in US treasuries as the yield goes down by the price hikes.
This possibility of downgrading the rating has been in the works for some time and now that it has come about, it is like a wet firecracker, to me anyway.
Since the rating is only an opinion, everyone had the time to make his own opinion since the last few months. There is so much money out there, that there isn't anywhere to go beside US treasuries. Only the long Government Bond holders are at risk which means all the US banking system.
The state of the US economy is more crucial than ratings since it means if the US sees a double dip recession, it will take all economies with them besides Brazil, Canada, and India which are doing relatively well this year.

It depends a lot on China's economic performance and if they do let their currency appreciate
on the market.
If QE3 comes about, will it go to investors or the consumers or to companies to create investments that will turn out in future jobs? If the money goes to investors, forget about a recovery. If it goes to consumers, perhaps there is a chance of slowly contributing to the recovery. If it goes to small and medium firms, it will create jobs so badly needed.

STOCKS TUMBLES AGAIN-Noon E.S.T.
The only good news is that if the stock market goes down again by 3 to 4%, commodities are also coming down. Energy commodities are all down by close to 3% and the WTI 4%. All Agricultural commodities are down as well, except for gold which is up by the same percentage.
This is turning out like a ''big correction.''
I'm anxious to see how the day is going to end up. Selling generates margin calls and margin calls generate more selling. Where do you think this going?

SLIPPERY WHEN WET
After the market close today, the Dow had slipped by 5.5% the S&P of 6.6% and NASDAQ of 6.9% and BAC of 20%, the one holding most Government Bonds and the TSX of 500 points as well and Europe and Asia by the same percentage. What the market didn't need was the downgrading of Fanny Mae and Freddie Mac Companies, the two mortgage companies belonging to the Government.
Everything is not that grim, particularly for the one that shorted Bank of America.
All energy commodities futures are in the red; The Brent down 4.4% and WTI down 6.6%.

All agricultural commodities are in the red as well. Gold and silver up: inevitably.

Some are upset by the downgrading like the President and Warren Buffet and others which believe it is all academic and with no real substance because Standard & Poor's doesn't read things right.

AUGUST 9-2011
There is smart money in the wings, backstage, waiting to grab some stocks as losers are licking their wounds from this week and last week selloff. Stock index shows a 12 P/E from a 16 P/E. The dismal 1.3% growth in GDP for the last quarter scared investors thinking that there might be a double dip recession underway.
The S &P future Index which opens before the stock market is showing a sign that stocks are getting under value and it is time to buy again. There is always money out there from ''bottom feeders.''
The S&P rating confirmed that the US will be in trouble again particularly if debt ceiling is increased to $ 16 trillion and revenues will be hard to come by if the economy is not picking up steam.
Money flew into currencies yesterday and still in US treasury since it is a safe haven for most.
Bernanke's QE 3 is on the verge of getting realised creating stimulus trying to escape a double dip recession.
I think Bernanke's buying Government securities from the banks to create liquidity should come with a condition; the funds will be used to lend to corporations with expansion programs. If this sounds too Keynesian, it is much better than letting banks trying to top profits by speculating on different markets and not creating the jobs needed.

The relief of retail gas is not as quick to come by since it is at $3.67 a gallon down .03 cents and 135.4 cents a liter, down .046 cents while the WTI is at $81.50 and Brent at $104.00 It doesn't have the same momentum as it did when going up. Most commodities in the futures market are seeing green today as early markets tell us.

WEEK OF AUGUST 8 TO 12-2011. THE ROLLER COASTER WEEK

The roller coaster ride of last week, the stock market going down 400 points in a day and then back up 300 points is not unusual based on bad economic figures making the future quite dismal. The major point after my August 9 comments is that the commodities' market followed very closely the stock market with major swings as well is **the *proof*** that there is a lot of speculation money in the commodities' market that shouldn't be there.

The increase back up on markets is not that optimists are gaining ground over pessimists; it is simply traders covering their short positions.

Turkey, Greece, Spain, France and Belgium banned ''short selling'' on their respective markets because they want to stop these erratic's movements.

If Bernanke wants to liquidate again the economy with QE3, he better put a condition that this new money should be lent to small and medium size company, not to speculate on the markets.

I've made that point before that if banks and quasi banks don't want to lend to companies thinking they are too risky, the QE3 money will go in the stock and commodity' market again as it did for QE1-2.

I'm afraid that Mr. Bernanke was given the FINGER by the banking system and all other financial institutions which withheld the new money and used it for speculation and made us, the consumers, pay for the high prices of commodities for nothing. *The Royal Finger.*

CHAPTER TRHEE
WOOPS! OIL SPILLS

I guess the oil companies that are responsible for oil spills are easy targets to criticize because of the indisputable damage they do to the environment, to fishermen and costal people and wildlife.

I certainly don't want to rehash the stories because they are well known and documented and complex since they have both; the Exxon Valdez and BP Deepwater Horizon spills occupied dozens of lawyers and to this day. Reading the stories though makes it evident that there was human error on both counts. Either of neglect or omission pushed by time and cost or escaping maintenance is just short of malicious, just to increase profits.

My point is that a company is mainly a ''human component'' and thus should be treated as such in front of the courts and made responsible for damages and punitive damage. These externalities, expressed by Milton Friedman were of unimaginable scale. These ''external costs'' goes beyond the company expectations of doing business but they occur just the same, they are part of the risk. This is why corporations have to be responsible like citizens in view of the nature of their activity and space on earth. Governments cannot be there all the time to see if regulations are followed or there are potential dangers in the prevalent activities. The culture of responsibility has to be from within. Company personnel are not liable for their individual actions since they obey instructions but they come from human managers which do make errors of judgement. If people were not there to make decisions, they wouldn't be needed. Thus, corporations are law binding citizens.

COAL ENERGY

Coal use is still widely around as a fossil fuel and I have to accept it reluctantly since I can't help to visualize the black cloud coming out of coal burning. I thought it was for countries like Hungary, Bulgaria, Poland and all the other countries ending with ''tan'' where primitive heating energy is still in use and all of its citizens started to look like they literally came out of a coal mine.

China, the new super power is a great user of coal and imports coal mainly from Australia. Since December 2009, coal prices have gone upward and downward to an August low of $97 m.t. fluctuating from $89 m.t. and today, December 2010 to $123. m.t. China is also the third biggest world producer.

We are aware of the flood in Australia and how it does hinder economic activity all around.

I am curious to see if there is *per se* really a cause for a 26% increase due to the flood or is it just a market reaction to disaster and the market specialists are profiting from the panic on energy supply. The reason of my thinking is that coal is not mined and extract in cities and the supply shouldn't be affected, only transportation disability can create some drawbacks. Let see if my skepticism is warranted.

Looking at the flood results on the news and on the net, it is by no means a small disaster. Through 17 rivers, Queensland has been debased by the 25 ft. wave which went through way out the inland and paralyzed most communication and transportation facilities. Four out of the six ports in Queensland were out of commission leaving only two in New South Wales.

151

The major city affected was RockHampton were some major coal activity went through.

The effect of the flood will take months if not years to soak up and to be brought back to its normalcy. My question is not the level of the catastrophe and how much damage it will do in the short and the long term my qualm is the price of coal exports on a world level. Is the 26% increase in world price is immediately justified since there is some other coal producers and exporters which could fill the gap of Australia's export?

True that Australian export almost 97% of its production or reserve, making this country a major player but *not the only player* and *not the major producer* in the world.
The US is the major producer followed by Russia and China and India and then comes Australia with 9% of world reserve followed by a hundred of other countries.

Let's distinguish between Recoverable Reserve (**RR**) and Production (**P**) of coal.

Proved Recoverable Reserve Coal at 2008 (million tonnes)

	Bituminus	anthracite	Subbituminus	Lignite	%
U.S	108,501	98,618	30,176	237,295	27.6
Russia	49,088	97,472	10,450	157,010	18.2
China	62,200	33,700	18,600	114,500	13.3
Australia	37,100	2,100	37,200	76,500	8.9
India	56,100	0	450	64,600	7.0

Production of Coal by country and year (Million tonnes)

	2006	2007	2008	2009	Share%	Life Reserve
China	2380	2526.0	2782.0	3050.0	45.6	38 years.
USA	1053.6	1040.2	1062.8	973.2	15.8	245

India	447.3	478.4	521.7	557.6	6.2	105
E U	595.5	593.4	587.7	536.8	4.6	35
Australia	385.3	399.0	401.5	409.2	6.7	186
Russia	309.2	314.2	326.5	298.1	4.3	500+

Export of Coal by Country and year. (Million short tons)

Country	2006	2007	2008	2009	Share in %
Australia	255.0	268.5	278.0	288.5	26.5
Indonesia	192.0	221.0	228.2	261.4	24.0
Russia	103.4	112.2	115.4	130.9	12.0
Colombia	68.3	74.5	74.7	75.7	6.9
South Africa	75.8	72.6	68.2	73.8	6.8
USA	51.2	60.6	83.5	60.4	5.5
China	86.5	75.4	68.8	38.4	3.5

Imports of Coal by country and Year (million short tons)

Country	2006	2007	2008	2009	Share %
Japan	199.7	2001.0	206.0	182.1	17
China	42.0	56.2	44.5	151.9	14.5
South Korea	84.1	94.1	107.1	109.9	10.6
India	52.7	29.6	70.9	76.7	7.4
Taiwan	69.1	72.5	70.9	64.6	6.2
Germany	50.6	56.2	55.7	45.9	4.4
U.K	56.8	48.9	49.2	42.2	4.1

Source: Wikipedia Short tons are after triage.

There was a substantial increase in imports by China from 2008 to 2009 and a gradual export to China from Australia. It seems like the increase was filled by Russia and the US where the reserve is quite abundant.

I don't know if Japan, China and South Korea are unwilling to import coal from the US, but the later can fill up the supply chain quite easily. The US producers 27% of the world coal reserve and export only 5.5% on a world level and it has been said that it has a 245 life year supply.

This is of course looking at the big picture without consideration of the intrinsic quality of coal, if it is black coal or brown coal and its capacity (density) of fuel energy.

Over hall, I can honestly say that the unfortunate disaster which plagues Australia, brings only a *shift* in supply and not ''the supply at large''. I'm sure the world supply in the pipeline is able to furnish the coal needed for fuel and iron making around the world for months to come if not years. It is a question of *time lag* between reserves and final usage. I don't think this ''time lag'' justifies a 26% price increase on the world's markets. China is not running out since it is the third largest producer of coal and can easily increase production. Russia, the closes neighbour has +500 years of reserve. Some of the players in this market are taking some unearned excess profits, *giving us the finger, again.*
(It's not like we were going to run out of beer in a matter of weeks, that I would be worrisome somewhat.)

CHAPTER FOUR-

NEBULOUS DISCREPENCIES

Itwouldn't be fair because it is an easy target not mentioned the ENRON scandal which occurred in 2001. The story was well publicized because of its shear ''grandeur'' of the fraud and documented throughout by a book, a movie and many news articles. Just reading the summary on Wikipedia gives one an idea of the complexity of the file. Through a cobweb of companies offshore, the management was able to hide debt unscrupulously accumulated and the losses appeared as profits. I certainly don't want to recap the story one would have a better idea by reading the book. I just wanted to point out that it is astoundingly deceitful how human beings can act as corporate bandits out in the open under the name of greed and to the detriment of small investors and employees. Not that these executives were not making a nice living to begin with but lying openly to people of good faith, is disturbingly appalling. What surprises me is that the aftermath didn't change much the honesty level at the corporate level. Many other companies were caught doing the same thing, doctoring the books, and or having another set of books altogether. An old trick with only bigger numbers.

I don't want to sit in the ''sanctimonious high chair'' like a tennis judge but it seems like these companies operated like they were in Far West.

WorldCom and Lehman Brothers followed filling the front page with the same type of scandals.

Bernard Madoff followed suit in 2008 with his investment firm and other ''little Madoff'' using the Ponzi scheme (more on this later) came unveiling themselves with the same trick but with smaller amounts. There were a few in my province like Norbourg, Norshield and a few individuals operating under their own name as money managers, which stole millions from little old ladies just like Miss Daisies.

Not that fraud in business and stock manipulation is new. In the gold mining industry, falsifying the appraisal reports has been around since the gold rush in California and still today, geologist falsification is done all the time and expanded to other metal and precious stones. People find diamonds right underneath their feet sometimes!!!

Snake oil salesmen are still around, now they have MBA's from Harvard and law degrees not to mention accountants, the best seat in the house to rob corporations and individuals.

When given the opportunity, how many can stay honest and be lawful?

Veteran cops turn dirty when the opportunity arises by taking stolen money or valuable drugs.

And who can honestly say that they never sent a bill which was utterly inflated? Electricians, plumbers not to mention proverbial car mechanics overly charging for unneeded work.

Just yesterday, April 9, 2011 on W5 TV program (CDN) they were broadcasting about the annual test done by the Automobile Protector Association to evaluate car repair shops with a five year old car which have been checked and serviced by AAA and modified deliberately with a small problem like a loose battery to check the honesty of the suggested repairs.

The test was done in Toronto and Calgary with the same car with the same starting problem, the loose battery cable.

Among the 30 repair shops, 22 failed (73%) to find the exact problem and suggested other things to be done as opposed to tighten the battery cable.

Some came up with changing the battery which was checked before and of course was fine. Some came up with changing the spark plugs and were given the wrong ''old plugs'' to the customer and one came up with a change of breaks for a starting problem!!!

The highest bill was $2,200. for repairs and the most honest didn't charge anything to tighten the cable. Remember, 22 out of 30 deliberately gave *the customer the royal finger*.

Let me think! Ho yes, I almost forgot, who has the most money? Yeah! Governments.

From bailouts to subsidies to false billing, no interest loans and right out embezzlement from the treasury, exaggerated expenditures and write offs and dispensing influence for gratuities.

The major bailout from President Obama came to an end with another scandal. The executive bonus payout at the end of the year like nothing happened. The taxpayers were disbursed to pay for a new paint job on a company's Lear Jet during a recession, just adding insult to injury.

IT PAYS GOING TO PRISON

In a Bloomberg article, (July 6th.2011) California prison's physician got paid $838,706 including benefits and back salary. Other professionals, 9 out of 10 got paid over $500,000 for their services to the State prison in 2010, mostly doctors, psychiatrists and dentists.

Even in a prison, you can make money.

Governor Gerry Brown's salary is only $173,987.

OTHER FRONT PAGE SCANDALS

Even though I'm interested in energy and food prices and particularly future food prices, it is interesting to go back to some infamous scandals that occurred in 2002. It is easy to put the thumb down on people who managed such enormous schemes, but certainly not easy to decipher the how's and why's. The case of WorldCom presided by Bernard Ebbers is as complicated as a labyrinth full of cobwebs in the dark in a floorless cave. I think what is most fascinating is that communication companies handle things that are so intangible as much as their doctored financial reporting of 11 billion of income when there was no such thing.

It ended up in an 41 billion dollar bankruptcy, the largest ever reported in the history of the United States and Mr. Bernard Ebbers (a Canadian by the way) was convicted of 25 years in jail. The story his fascinating to read if one can understand it. (See the article of Santa Clara University written by Denis Moberg and Edwards Romar from UM Boston) where they make sense of it all.

To me what is fascinating is how a company can get away with it for so long with the SEC watching listed companies, big accounting firms that are supposed to audit companies, executives that are supposed to do things right and know where everything is going and internal accounting, plus bankers watching cash flow and brokerage analysts recommending the stock to investors. This adds up to hundreds of watchdogs and nobody barks.

How come all these people didn't understand what was going on or everyone was *in on it*, accepting bribes? Bigger is certainly better for fraud when everything becomes so undecipherable and incomprehensible that most become mentally challenged, beyond their scope of expertise.

Others made headlines as well, like Tyco and Lehman Brothers were ''bigger'' was synonymous to invincible. ''Too big to fail'' seems an absurd cliché now, after horrific disasters.

The only ones which came up on top were the big lawyers. Lots of work for them.

I wish I would have been a Wall Street lawyer where there is plenty of work to go around, so it seems.

CAPOCHINO INDEX

The other drastic increase recently was the retail price of coffee. Like most of us, it is my morning fuel to get me going and I'm probably ready to pay any price for the first cup of coffee. Living in the northern part of North America, coffee is as important as premium gasoline. A walk in Vancouver near Stanley Park will testify how important the warm beverage is crucial by the number of coffee shops available. People walk with their coffee cups in hand they take the bus with their coffee cups drive with their coffee cups, even sit outside in the rain with their coffee cups.

In my city, in the last ten years or so, coffee shops have replaced bars, literally. Students have adopted the coffee shops for libraries and a place to chat online, do their homework and to meet with other students. Coffee as dislodged the draft beer, a healthier choice.

When the newspapers stipulate the bad crops are the reason, (either droughts or floods or frost) the culprit of rising prices like any other farmed product, the price increase if reflected the next day. I have no doubts that farming is a risky business subject to the whims of the weather unpredictable ravage that affect supply in a giving year but I'm always surprised by the announcement of bad crops let say in Brazil, (the largest producers) influences the price the next day (so to speak) or the next few weeks on the shelves of retailers. Again, it is the anticipation of limited supply that triggers a hike in prices and not the limited supply *per se* on that day. People stock up thinking it will go higher and the demand immediately increases the price.

I really don't know the time lag between harvesting coffee beans and having a cup of coffee on my table but I'm sure it is not a matter of weeks. I'm sure though that the farmer is not getting the immediate price increase that shows up at my grocery store. The retailer will say," I have to pay more to my wholesaler" and the wholesaler will say, "I have to pay more to my importer," and the importer will say, "I have to pay more to my roaster" but the farmer, the big looser of all, has nothing because he is short of crops to sell if there is a frost or damage to the crop.

Market psychology is at work, thinking bad crops equal higher prices and consumer are willing to pay. Same as any other commodity, there is fear build up and some traders are making excess profits with fear and natural disasters.

With the 7.80 million metric tons produced in the world by a total ten major exporting countries (2006), and all the coffee in the pipeline which goes through *five* different hands, besides the Mercantile Exchange of futures contracts, and profit taking on five levels, don't tell me that the farmers themselves receives compensation for their losses of revenues because of the bad crop. Not long ago the farmers were selling at a lost ($ 0.74 per pound) before establishing a floor price of $1.20 lbs. Coffee production is labour intensive and the farmer does most of the labour, the others are just roasters and traders.

(Source: Wikipedia Encyclopedia)

Let's look more deeply at the 2010 price increase if we can find *the market finger.*

Like any world trading commodity, the economics of coffee market are complex.

There are the cash market and the futures market. The cash market is for users and the futures market are for hedger-users and investors or speculators. Hedging is simply to confirm price at a set quantity for the future in order to stabilize prices or prevent market drastic increase if there is a shortage of the underlying commodities. Speculators are people not interested in taking delivery of the set commodity, but simply making a profit on trades by selling the contract before expiry date.

Needless to say that the futures market is an anticipation of what is coming ahead on the supply side. Either regular supply, increase in supply, shortage of supply. It's either one of the three.

There are grades of coffee quality as well which trade at different prices. Brazil produces one third of the world market. So, whatever happens in Brazil, prices swings are expected to follow.

In an article dated June 14, 2010 in the Guardian U.K saying that coffee price rose 20% in a week based on reduction of supply of 20% in Vietnam being the second world exporter. I was in Vietnam in 2010 and I have to admit the coffee is excellent if not exceptional in coffee shops. I didn't know Vietnam exported coffee until that day but it is mainly Robusta coffee for instant coffee fabrication.

Compared to Brazil, it is still a small exporter.

The International Coffee Organization (ICO) said that green coffee export dropped by 8.1% during October to April. The Robusta coffee price (said to be lower in quality) increase 20% in three days. It is mentioned that traders were buying to cover their short positions on the market.

Vietnam exported 0.85 million metric tons in 2006 versus Brazil exported 2.59 million metric tons. Vietnam export is 14.5% of world market versus Brazil 38% and Colombia 12.3%.

The WNYC –January 2011 reports that demand for coffee is exceeding supply since more people want to drink coffee like Americans do from emerging countries like India and China. Some people are switching from tea to coffee.

Poor crops in Brazil, hording in Vietnam to increase stock, virus on leafs in Colombia, increases in world demand are the main causes for the increase in retail prices says the newspapers.

KCU11 - Coffee (ICEUS) - Daily OHLC Chart
Op:240.60, Hi:243.70, Lo:240.10, Cl:241.35
Vol: 3,770

This being said and being acceptable as an argument, when looking at the figures more closely, I see hype on prices justified by overly negative reports in the headlines in the newspapers. The disease on crops in Colombia is real but Colombia is a small contributor to world export so is Vietnam. The reduction of production in Vietnam is small in comparison of Brazil.

Of course as I mentioned before, there are different kinds of coffee at different prices.

We have to divide the two main ones being; Arabica and Robusta

I would like to know how much production is affected, how much the reserves are affected and the change in the world market before the increase in retail price.

From the Monthly Coffee Market Report of December 2010 by the International Coffee Organization (ICO), the same organization stated before, they are at least 25 exporting countries in the world market. Seven in Africa, six in Asia & Oceania and seven in Mexico & Central America, five in South America. The news focuses only on Brazil, Colombia and Vietnam.

I'm interested in the price increase since the year 2008-2009-2010 and 2011, mainly in the latter part of the last six months of 2010 when the price increase was substantial.

On the production side;

PRORODUCTION IN EXPORTING COUNTRIES (In thousand bags)

Crop year commencing

	2008	2009	2010	% 2010 & 2009
TOTAL	128,587	122,855	134,633	9.6
Africa	15,933	15,655	18,140	15.9
Asia & Oceania	34,829	36,768	35,735	-2.8
Mexico & Central	17,519	16,911	18,174	7.5
South America	60,305	53,520	62,584	16.9

In the latter zone of production, Brazil had an increase in production from 2007 to 2010 of 21.9% and Colombia of 11.1% and Vietnam a decrease of -1.1%.

I wish I could stop my argument right now because based on gross production there are no reason for a rapid price increase since production was increased in all regions except by Asia & Oceania. Let's look at the *demand side* and the *bad news* that contributed to the price increase. Again, let me reiterate the fact that, market perceptions affect prices, not actual present reality. This is of course, is the premise of the book. This 8 page report by the ICO goes into the eye of my inquiry. Market fundamentals;

'' Crop year 2010/11 has been affected by adverse weather conditions which have caused some delay in harvesting and transportation. Total production in 2010/11 is estimated at 134.6 million bags, a rise of 11.8 million bags (9.6%) over the previous year. Most of this increase will be in Arabia production, which is expected to grow by 10.8 million bags (almost 15%). Robusta production is expected to rise by just under 1 million bags (nearly 2%) It should be noted that crop year 2010/11 is a high production year in Brazil and recent estimates by the coffee authorities indicate a total production of 48.1 million bags.

Nevertheless, unfavorable weather conditions and coffee tree disease seem to have reduced production potential in some other exporting countries. More specifically, an increase of 7% is expected in Mexico and Central America region, mainly due to increase production in El Salvador, Guatemala, Honduras and Mexico. In Asia and Oceania, production is expected to decrease slightly in Vietnam and significantly in Indonesia as a consequence of adverse weather. In Colombia, an increase in production is expected, however, the coffee industry is still experiencing difficulties, particularly as a result of the outbreak of disease, especially coffee leaf rust, which may delay a return to the country normal production levels.''

The last published number was an increase of 11.1% in Colombia in 2009/2010 of 9,000 bags in total production of 134,633 million bags.

'' African production is expected to increase by around 16% mainly as a result of continued high performance with Ethiopia and increases in other countries.''

Ethiopia produced 7,450 million bags and Colombia produced an increase of 11.1% to 9,000 bags in 2010. Based on those figures, I see more an anxiety reaction of the delayed crop and rust on coffee leafs in Colombia which represents only 6.6% of world production.

Let's continue our quote from the article;

'' In Brazil, crop year 2011/12 will begin in the next few months and production will be lower in accordance with the biennial production cycle for Arabica. The level of this decrease may, however, be reduced due to advances in agricultural practices that should make it possible to reduce pronounced fluctuation in production for one year to the next. Initial estimate published by the Brazilian authorities indicate total production between 41.9 and 44.7 million bags, the highest level recorded for low production in the biennial year cycle that characterizes Arabica production in Brazil.''

When you write words like; nevertheless and however or it may in a statement, it means that there is another side which counterbalance the view. I think this later point counter balances itself out.

The market fundamentals article ends this way:

''In the case of crop year 2009/10, the estimated total production level has been revised upward to just under 123 million bags.''

This end the article on an up-tick on the production side.

'' Export in November totaled 7.7 million bags, bringing the total volume exported the first eleven months of the calendar year 2010 to 87.1 million bags against 88.3 million bags in the same period in year 2009, a fall of 1.4%. Brazilian exports were the highest recorded for the month of November.''

The decline in percentage seems to be a manageable number without influencing the price.

'' Data on consumption in the five leading importing countries (France, Germany, Italy, Japan and the United States) indicated a total consumption of 37.3 million bags during the period January to September 2010 compared to 36.5 million bags for the same period in 2009. It should be noted that domestic consumption in Brazil is expected to continue to grow at a fast pace.''

The increase of imports from Europe and the US is only 0.8 million bags, not something to push prices upward. The last statement should be backed by a number because it is worded in a way that Brazilians just discovered coffee lately. The economics of Brazil are changing, people spend more but to a point of creating a surge on demand in the producing country when people have been drinking coffee for a hundred years or more? I don't think so. You don't drink more coffee because of prosperity. Population growth I believe, but not prosperity. An increase in Champagne drinking I would believe.

There was an increase of 4.0% from 2008 to 2009 in local consumption. There was a large increase in Vietnam in local consumption of 18.3%. This, I believe since Vietnam is *so poor*, that an increase of disposable income would influence consuming habits in coffee drinking .

I was in HCM city in 2010 and people are literally fighting for survival. When you eat snakes, I think you are in survival mode.

Funny enough that world consumption has increased in producing countries by 3.1% and there was a reduction of -3.2% in importing countries in 2008/2009. That equals out.

To reiterate the point of local consumption in exporting countries, Brazil consumed per capita 5.64 kilograms in 2009 from 5.48 in 2008 and 5.34 in 2007 and 5.14 in 2006. The increase is steady but certainly not dramatic or worth to mention. In Vietnam, per capita consumption went through to 0 .82 kilograms in 2009 from 0.70 in 2008 and 0.67 and 2007 and 0.58 in 2006.

In percentage, (18%) is high but certainly not in quantity. Most exporting countries consumed much less coffee than importing countries, except for Brazil. In comparison, Canada consumed 5.88 kilograms per capita in 2009 and the US consumed 4.09 kilograms per capita. The cold weather certainly explains the difference between the two countries but pale in comparison to Luxembourg of 27.40 kilograms, Finland was 11.92 k. per capita and 8.92 k for Norway. Drinking five times more coffee (Luxembourg) than Canadians seems like a ''sport'' more than merely regular consumption.

Peculiar enough that *retail prices* September 2008 to September 2010 have declined in Europe even in Luxembourg (7.4%) and stable in the USA for the same period. The rapid increase in retail prices did occur later in 2010.

It's worth noticing that retail prices are different if one speak of ''coffee shop prices'' and ''grocery prices''. In coffee shops, the profit margin is quite high to begin with (300%) since it is service included, meaning that they can absorb more a price increase of the raw product (not ground) as oppose to the coffee in a can at a grocery store. Coffee shops can't increase their prices so easily since there is competition to consider and customer loyalty.

The conclusion of the report says: ''that the current supply/demand structure has reinforced the continued firmness in prices throughout 2010 and that current development in market fundamentals suggest that prices will remain firm during 2011. In addition to the tight supply situation, both consumption and low stock level is likely to continue to support prices.''

This report was written in December 2010 and is probably shy of reporting the last substantial increase in retail prices and the futures market. I don't think they would be a more recent report since it does take time to compile the figures.

My conclusion based on the later events reported in the newspapers of, frost and virus on the coffee leaf and mediocre crops in Brazil and increase consumption in Brazil *doesn't warrant* a substantial increase in retail prices because it doesn't tell us how it affected the crop if any. I really believe that the ''bad news'' influenced the futures market, like all speculative markets, creating a fictitious scare, pushing the futures market to over $2.00 a pound. Don't forget that traders or speculators profit from ''high and low of markets, whatever direction it is going. Traders and hedgers just don't simply wait markets to go up to make money, they make money on the fluctuations. A stable market is not good for traders, fluctuations are great.

You have puts and call options of contracts and one can sell short as well. In the last stock market debacle, some people made billions shorting stocks. Shorting BP Oil stock was a good bet. People do make money on bad news.

The fluctuations are integral of a market and a bit of bad news will affect markets, creating fluctuations, thus, opportunities for traders.

I think they are jittery traders that see opportunities in bad news and react quickly making our lives, the consumer, just more expensive. I think there is a *finger in the coffee market* .

MARCH 21-2011-CNN NEWS & BLOMBERG NEWS

In a recent article, Mr. Richard Girardot from Nespresso Inc. mentioned that ''coffee will decline because it is overvalued by 50%. Markets have been driving upward by speculators and not fundamentals.''

I'm glad to see that someone in the business agrees with me that speculators are at the core of increases when weather news are released and with a little help of journalists with fatal titles on the potential influence on supply, drive prices upward without alterations of supply.

CEREALS CRUNCH?

Ever since I was a kid I enjoyed having a bowl of crunchy cereals in the morning. I don't know if it is because of the crunch sound it makes while you are chewing them or because it is easy to prepare or this ritual is simply comforting, bringing you back at the years when you were a kid.

In the last two years the price of cereals has gone up considerably much to my surprise living in a country which produces masses of cereals and even have been called the ''granary of the world.''

If there is something that went upward in price, almost by the week, is the price of cereal boxes. So much that I'm changing my habit from box cereals, mostly granola types of raw uncooked oatmeal in a bag (porridge) and adding my own delicacies like raisins and dry cranberries and bananas and fruit yogurt. I think I've curtailed the price increase of my breakfast.

If we experienced a substantial price increase in North America, I can't imagine its effect on countries that are not producing it and have to import it from us. I'm not ready to fold and say, ''that is inflation'' and close the file particularly after the years of 2008, 2009 and 2010 were recession years. What is going on?

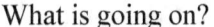

If you are confused as much as I am about the different kinds of cereals, to know what is the difference between oats, barley, whole wheat, grain, flax, buckwheat grits, rye flakes, cornmeal, millet, sunflower seeds, yeast, poppy seeds, sesame seeds, cracked sorghum, soy and flower and rice, lets' begin with the definition of my 14 cereal bread.

If I was asked to distinguish from all these cereals, I would be honestly stuck for an answer.

There must be some major cereals and some minor, meaning some are used more than others in all kinds of product like bread and some more popular than other for their taste.

The first distinction Wikipedia Encyclopedia makes is between breakfast cereals and grains.

Grain can be used naturally or processed like in bread for instance and commercial breakfast cereals. They have been known for their nutritional benefits and part of fiber intake and a balanced diet. In their natural form, whole grains are a great source of vitamins, minerals, fat and proteins. Cereal grains are grown in greater quantities and provide more food energy worldwide than any type of crop; they are therefore staple crops.

It is good to know who produces which grain and what they are used for and how much they contribute to nutrition. Like **maize** for instance (corn in North America or Indian corn) is not solely used for human consumption as we know, it is used for livestock and now, for extracting ethanol for a by-product of fuel. **Rice** is the primary cereal of tropical and some temperate regions. It is the primary food of China and all around Asia and Indonesia.

Wheat is the primary cereal of temperate regions. It has a worldwide consumption but it is a staple food of North America, Europe, Australia and New Zealand. **Barley** is grown for malting and livestock on land too poor or too cold for wheat.

Sorghum is an important food in Asia and Africa and popular worldwide for livestock.

Millet belongs in a group which is similar but distinct cereal which forms an important staple food in Asia and Africa. **Oats** was formerly the staple food of Scotland and popular

worldwide for livestock. **Rye** is important in cold climates and **Triticale** is a hybrid of wheat and rye, grown similar to rye. **Fonio** comes in various varieties which are grown as food crops in Africa. **Buckwheat** is a pseudocereal, as it is a Polygonacea and not a Poaceae or Gramineae used in Eurasia. Major uses include various pancake and groats.
Quinoa is a pseudocereal grown in the Andes .
They are other cereals which are grown but have little impact on cereals worldwide.
Maize, wheat and rice together accounted for 87% of all grain production worldwide and 43% of all food calories in 2003 while the production of oats and rye have drastically fallen from their 1960s levels. (Source: Wikipedia)

This information serves as a base in order to get to the price hike of cereal on the shelves. I know that price increase is a word used which equals inflation, but is it *cost push* increase? Is it *demand pull* increase? Governmental induced by *limiting farmer's quotas*? Influences of natural disasters? Like *droughts* and *flooding*? Or *importing inflation* from other countries like China? We shall find out.

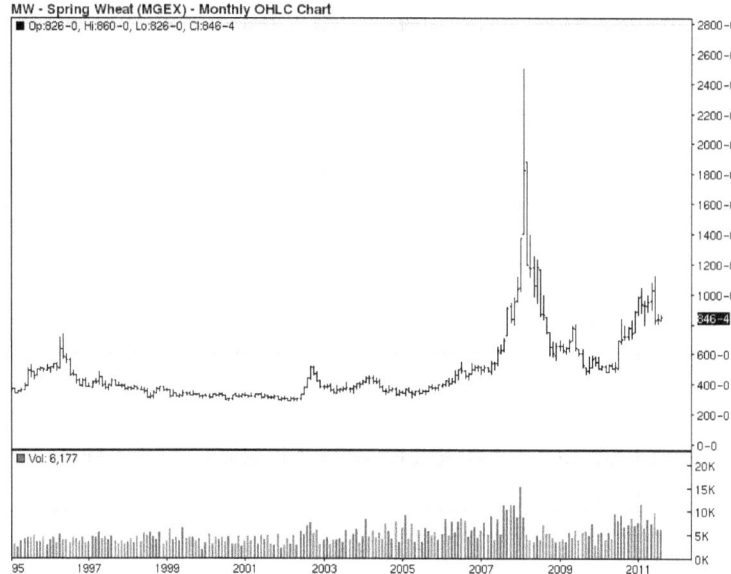

MW - Spring Wheat (MGEX) - Monthly OHLC Chart

The CPI, revisited

In general, when we define inflation we are referring to the
consumer price index (CPI) published by the Bureau of
Labour and Statistics on a monthly basis. Before going
anywhere with the CPI, the bureau itself explains at length
what is the CPI and what it includes and what it excludes.
Most analysts are skeptical in the Government published
figures and are always ready to have a contrarian view no
matter what.

To simplify matters, we are going to take the CPI-U for what it
is. It is an estimate basket of price change of food and services
bought by household at an average urban location.

We are aware that price varies upon location (transportation)
and depending on exactly what we consume. Some CPI
figures are released with energy cost and also excluded.

Without belabouring the point because it is not the scope of this book to evaluate the CPI, we acknowledge that it is an *estimate* of an *average*. Suffice to say that we give the CPI the weight it deserves, a starting point for discussion.

The CPI-U in 2000 to 2010 was a graph (All Items) as follows;

2000-3.6 %
2001-3.0 %
2002-1.5 %
2003-3.25%
2004-2.0 %
2005-3.0 %
2006-5.0%
2007-3.0%
2008-5.0%
2009-(2.0%)
2010-3.1%
(Source: DLS. Gov.)

We are not interested in the exact or absolute percentage we are interested in the fluctuations between years as long as the numbers were computed the same way. Numbers are relative and not absolute, unless you're counting the Van Trap family. Under the years of observation we notice a high percentage of 5.0% in 2008 and a drastic cut in 2009 of minus 2.0% (in recession time) and a large movement of five points back in 2010.

We did acknowledge in recent pages that the gasoline cost was at their peak in 2008 and crude oil at $147. a barrel.

The CPI takes the energy cost in consideration, but it is not all energy prices which go up. We are not considering electricity, coal, nuclear, natural gas, waste (or wood) burning and solar and wind turbines. Some forms of energy do compete with fossil fuel like coal, but gas and electricity need the infrastructure for delivery. In some household in Canada for instance, people rely on tri-energy (heating oil-natural gas-electricity) since it is an important part of winter. Some uses their wood stove on top of it whenever they feel it is more convenient or other sources are not available.

During the year 2010 some commodities have increased considerably and I'm afraid expected to go up in 2011 as well, according to some analysts. In a recovering year after a recession, it is surprising to see prices go up so rapidly.
CORN: under $4.00 a bushel to over $6.00. A 60.83% increase.
SOYBEANS: under $10. a bushel to $14.00. A 44.6% increase.
WHEAT: from $5.00 a bushel to $8.00. A 44.74% increase.
BARLEY: from $145 M.T. to $186.00 M.T. A 25.75% increase.
CRUDE OIL: $80 to $70 to $94 a barrel. A 20% increase.
NATURAL GAS: $5.50 (millions BTU) to $4.59 negative increase.
GOLD: from $1100 (troy ounce) to $1400
COFFEE: from below $1.40 pd. to $2.30 a 63.60% increase.
SUGAR: from .30 to .15 to back .35 pd. a 19.05% increase.
LIVE CATTLE; 28.26% increase.
FEEDER CATTLE: 26.0% increase.
PORK BELLIES: 21.77 % increase.
Source: CNN.com

ZS - Soybeans (CBOT) - Monthly OHLC Chart
Op:1354~2, Hi:1369~0, Lo:1354~2, Cl:1368~2

We can see why my breakfast is quite more expensive than it was in 2009.

It was not because of the crude oil increased that these commodities rose substantially since crude oil increased only 20%, well under the commodities. It would have had to be an increase quite a bit more substantial than the underlying commodity to be a major factor of the rise in prices. We can't blame oil for everything.

Commodity prices are a concern around the world where people find it impossible to make ends meet by the increasing percentage of disposable income spent on food. There are signs showing in England of people unrest and Egypt wants to change government because of the increase of commodity prices. Is the crisis in Egypt the first around the world where people are fed up paying an increasing high price for food? There was a street demonstration in Jordan recently where people want a new government and the king obliged. Is the

175

financial bailout of the US institutions is going to create hyperinflation where all commodities are going to double or triple in price or more?

We can confirm by looking at the Indices from December 2009 to December 2010.
CPI from 138 to 170
COMMODITY AGRICULTURAL RAW MATERIAL INDEX: from 110 to 150
COMMODITY FUEL (ENERGY) INDEX; 136 TO 166
COMMODITY FOOD & BEVERAGE INDEX: 144 to 177
COMMODITY FOOD PRICE INDEX: from 140 to 175
CRUDE OIL PRICES INDEX: 140 to 169
COAL, AUSTRALIA THERMAL COAL MONTHLY PRICES: from $89 to $123
CRUDE OIL DUBAI FATEH MONTHLY PRICES: $74 to $89
CRUDE OIL WEST TEXAS INTERMIDIATE (WTI) MONTHLY PRICES: $74 to $89.
Source: INDEX Mundi.com-IMF.
Some comments on the site;

Indian food prices (corn) have hit the highest level for a year, 18% rise annually and said to influence food prices all around the world. (January 2011)

BACK AT THE FARM

In order to get to the bottom of this, we begin with the farmers' prices and see which information lies on the ground to find when and why it all started.
As I thought, farming statistics are plentiful and elaborate not to mention that deciphering them gets to be challenging. I feel that I'm standing in the middle of a corn field seven feet high and can't see where exactly where I'm standing.

Needless to say that the figures reported will be a summary of the summary.

The USDA describes agricultural commodity prices received by farmers on a monthly basis and marketing year, average received by farmers at the point of first sale for all grades and qualities of the commodity sold. Points of first sales by farmers range from bulk sales at the farm to pack and graded products delivered at the local market. For crops, the price refers to all sales, regardless of the year harvested. The average price concept is that price which would result from dividing the total dollars received by all farmers before any marketing charges are deducted from the total quantity sold. The description is quite lengthy but I state the most relevant facts which are in line with the objectives of this book.

INDEX NUMBERS of PRICES RECIVED and PAID BY FARMERS,

Annual average, United States, 2001-2008

	2001-	2002-	2003-	2004-	2005-	2006-	2007-	2008
	Prices received (1990-92=100)							
All farm products	102	98	106	118	114	115	136	149
All Crops	99	105	110	115	110	120	142	168
Food Grains	91	104	109	120	111	134	186	258
Feed Grains & Hay	91	100	104	110	95	109	152	206
Oil-bearing Crops	80	88	107	134	106	100	137	202
Commer. Veg.	133	137	137	126	130	136	158	151
Pot. & Dry Beans	98	129	104	102	109	125	126	161

    Other Crops   112   114   113   113   113   116
118   123
(Source: USDA. Mannib.cornell.edu/usda)

Index numbers don't mean anything unless they are compared
year to year to see if they increase, decrease or remained
stable. In this case, (too bad we haven't the 2009-2010
numbers yet) we see a substantial increase in Food Grains
beginning in 2006 to 2008.
If we remember the CPI movement for those years, in 2005
the CPI was about 3% in 2006 at 5.0%, fell from 2007 to 3.0%
went back up in 2008 to over 5% and shoot down in 2009 to
minus 2% and back up to over 3% in 2010.
It is noticeable that All Crops were down in 2005 from 2004
and Oil –bearing crop as well. So, the bench mark increase
was more acceptable since it started from a lower base. We
can observe the *doubling* in price of Food Grains from 2004 to
2008 .

The expenses of running a farm are like any other business. If
costs are over your net profits, you create a loss. For the same
years as above;
Prices paid by farmers for Commodities and Services .

INDEX OF PRICES OF OPERATING COST
2001-02-03-04-05-06-07-08 + I+ T+ Wages:
123   124   128   134   142   150   161   184
Feed 109 112 114   121   117   124 149   191
Livestock & Poultry
111   102   109   128   138   134   121   135
Seed: 132 142 154   158   168   182   208   254
Fertilizer 123 108 124 140   164   176   216   375

Agricultural Chemicals
121   119   121   121   123   128   129   139

Fuels	121	115	140	165	216	239	264	372
Farm Supplies & Repairs								
124	127	130	134	140	145	150	153	
Autos & Trucks								
118	116	111	114	114	112	111	109	
Farm Machinery								
144	148	151	162	173	182	191	204	
Building Materials								
121	122	124	134	142	152	155	164	
Farm Services								
120	120	125	127	134	140	146	154	
Rent								
117	120	123	126	129	141	148	163	

The highlights are sharp movement from one year to the next, either on the *decrease* like Livestock & Poultry in the year 2006 to 2007. A sharp *increase* of seed cost in the years 2007-2008 and *a substantial increase* in Fuels in from 2005, 2006-2007-2008 while Autos & Trucks *decreased* in 2006, 2007, 2008.

The rest of the numbers show a regular increase.

The items which decreased in cost are less significant than the major increase in Fuel, Seeds and Fertilizer. In other words, exogenous factors are to blame being outside of the farmer's control. Cars and Trucks expenses can always be delayed as much as livestock purchases can be delayed, which they did since it shows a decrease in price, thus in expenditures.

With four sets of numbers we can make a conclusion about cost push inflation by fertilizers chemicals (potash) and fuel. As we saw previously, crude oil prices were not induced by limited supply or imports, since the demand was steady but the Reserve side showed a substantial increase. I suspect the high increase in Feed Grain was to do the fact that farmers were producing below their operating cost and had to pass on the increase in 2009-2010 based in the year before, 2008.

I believe the *Invisible Finger* was at work, the gouging of multi-international companies (fertilizers-pesticides-GM seeds-fuel) which affected the base of our economy; farmed products.

In a recent article titled; The Great Beyond: Food prices hit record highs with NO end in sight, in TOPIX.COM, dated January 6 - 2011, '' World food prices reached a new record high last month exceeding the 2008 peak that triggered riots in a number of countries, the UN's Food and Agriculture Organization (FAQ) reports.

The Food Price Index which covers dairy products, meat, sugar, cereals and oilseeds, averaged 214.7 points at the end of December 2010, up almost 4.2% from 206 points a month earlier and slightly above the previous peak of 213.5 points in June 2008. This was the highest it had reached since the index was created in 1999. Sugar, cereals and oil were the driving force in the rise, the report says. The cause was droughts in Russia and ''many other unexpected developments that hit crops around the world''. FAQ economist Absolresa Abbassian told the BBC.

It is certain droughts and floods affects agricultural products and the result of their crops but have you noticed how rapidly the prices goes up right after you hear it on the news? One can- not tell me that from *land* to *mouth*, that we are talking about days, even months of time lag. There is such a thing as harvesting, storing, drying, delivering, transforming, storing it in a different form, shipping to wholesalers, transportation to retailers, more storage, consumer's purchase, storing in cupboards or the basement or the garage and then to the table. I don't really know how much time we are talking about that we have in reserve of all foods but it is not certainly a few days. Price hikes do follow quite rapidly. I call it: *psychology of markets* as I mentioned before, (page 14) what people think will happen in the future. When people are worried or anxious about the future, it is a good time to act on their fears. They will pay a price increase because there is proof that we may run out. Markets react on chaos and fear, anticipating a grime future, at least a more expensive future. The contracts of future's market goes flying in Chicago.

SBV11 - Sugar #11 (ICEUS) - Daily OHLC Chart
Op:30.15, Hi:30.60, Lo:30.06, Cl:30.34
Vol: 15,084

In another article, it is mentioned that feed crop hikes affect livestock prices, thus prices at the grocery store for beef in Oklahoma. Again, the culprit is the drought in Russia and Africa and the flood in Australia. I'm sure that agricultural crops are an international market but I don't remember importing grain from Russia. I think North America (United States & Canada) produces more feed grain crops that we need. We are on the export side after all.

Trade statistics are plentiful and overwhelming to say the least, but I was able to come up with some statistics that serves the purpose of our last statement.

GRAIN: WORLD MARKETS AND TRADE
(USDA-Office of Global Analysis)
Regional Wheat Imports, Production, Consumption and Stocks. (Thousands Metric Tons)
Nov.   Dec.
TY Imports.

	2006/07-	07/08-	08/09- 20	09/10-2010/11	2010/11
North America					
	7,279	6,475	7,128	6,779	6,650	6,650
Former Soviet U.					
	5,986	6,105	6,502	5,415	7,375	7,325
Production					
North America					
	77,722	79,468	100,627	91,514	86,203	87,170
Former Soviet U.					
	84,904	92,447	115,453	113,839	83,030	82,630
Domestic Consumption					
North America					
	46,126	40,901	48,329	44,087	46,550	47,278
Former Soviet U.					
	72,551	74,856	76,316	80,250	84,975	84,350
Ending Stocks					
North America					
	19,690	13,108	24,729	35,144	28,772	29,711
Former Soviet U.					
	11,115	12,923	20,813	23,087	11,767	11,992

I've omitted from this report the other countries (12) to simplify our statement.

The Soviet Union Imports increased in the later year but production decreased as well (26%) and Ending Stock decrease from more than 50%.

In North America, Imports remained relatively stable but production decreases 16% in 2008/2009 to 2010/11 while domestic consumption was stable while Ending Stocks decrease

in 2009/2010 of 17%. Even if Soviet Union stock were down considerably, there has been no shortage since Ending stock were still at 11,992 (TMT) and North America produces twice as much as domestically consumes, making 40,000 (TMT) available for exports.

Why should North American prices of wheat have to go up again because of Russia drought?

Wheat is a single item, and all are computed like barley, rice, coarse grain, corn, sorghum, oats and rye.

All Grain Summary Comparison.
Corn- Wheat-Rice
Year: **2008/09 09/10 10/11- 08/09 09/10 10/11-2008/09 2009/10 2010/11**
Production
United States
    68.0   60.4   60.1   6.4   6.9   7.4   307.1
333.0   318.5
Other
    615.3   621.7 586.4 441.7 434.3 445.0 490.6 479.4
502.2

World Total
    683.3 682.1 646.5 448.1 441.2 452.4 797.8
812.4   820.7

Domestic Consumption
United States
  34.3   30.9   32.3   4.0   3.9   4.0   259.3
281.9 291.6
Other
600.7   618.8   631.3   431.3   431.3   447.2   520.4
527.4 543.2

World Total
635.0   649.7   663.5   435.3   435.2   451.2   779.7
809.3 834.8

Ending Stocks
United States
17.9   26.6   23.4   1.0   1.2   1.5   42.5
43.4   21.1
Other
148.3   170.1   153.4   90.7   94.2   93.2   104.8
103.8   108.9

World Total
166.2   196.7   176.6   91.7   95.3   94.8   147.3
147.2   130.0

TY Imports
United States
3.4   3.2   3.0   0.7   0.7   0.7   0.3
0.2   0.4
Other
136.9   128.4   119.4   26.1   27.8   27.6   82.1
89.7   89.5

World Total
140.3   131.6   122.3   26.8   28.5   28.3   82.5
89.9   89.9

TY Exports
United States

27.1	24.2	34.0	3.0	3.5	3.6	47.8	
49.9	50.0						
Others							
116.1	110.1	91.1	26.3	26.4	26.7	36.2	
42.8	42.0						
World Total							
143.2	134.3	125.1	29.2	29.9	30.3	84.0	
92.7	92.0						

Source: USDA

Note: Consumption in this table has not been adjusted for differences in marketing year imports and exports and therefore differs from global total shown elsewhere. (In TMT)

If we look at wheat, we noticed in the three years that production decrease in world total while production in the United States remained steady. Domestic consumption increased slightly in the United States while increased about 5% in the world. Ending stocks decreased in the US and in world total as well. Imports decrease in total while remaining the same in the US. Export increased considerably from the US about 45% while others and world total decreased.
The increase in consumption was offset by ending stock which had a good increase in the year 2009/10 (May).
 It seems that the US was able fill the gap of 10 t.m.t. while taking 20 t.m.t from reserve to compensate for the 30 t.m.t. increase in consumption. Ending stock in 2010/11 remained high relative to 2008/2009.
I don't see the reason for a sharp increase in prices since the ending stock was able to provide easily the increase in consumption.
Rice in not a big factor in regards to the United States since domestic consumption remained quite stable and minimum and production as well. Other countries take the bulk of production and consumption.

Corn production decreased in the US but increased in others and world total. Domestic consumption increased in the US and others as well and world total. Ending stocks decreases 50% by the US but increased slightly by others and decrease 11% on world total. Imports are small in the US but world total increased by close to 10% from year 2008/2009 to 2010/11.

Export remained stable for the US while increase by others and world total by more than 10%.

The decrease in production and the increase in consumption in the US were filled by ending stocks of 22 t.m.t. Neither imports nor exports were affected.

Since production from the US and world total increased by roughly 10% from 2008/09 to 2009/10 but decrease in the US only in 2010/11 and not by other and world total, I am lead to believe that production is easily controllable of 10 to 12% to meet the increase in demand.

There is a justification of a price increase but not substantial since the flexibility of production and some in ending stocks. The summary of production, domestic consumption and exports and imports and ending stocks shows that fluctuations are not drastic to warrant a sharp increase by international food firms. Again, as we saw in the crude oil sector, a slight decrease in reserve is immediately offset by a major increase in the retail market. I think that international companies are quick on the trigger to make sure bottom line profits stays up. Reserves are not at higher cost on the contrary, they would be at a lesser cost and selling them at higher prices, increases the profit margin.

Using corn to produce ethanol seems to be pushing the envelope, using food to produce energy, just seems an incongruent waste. Ethanol is used as a gasoline additive to reduce the price of gasoline over hall, but not if you increase the price of corn.

Money is better spent on hybrid cars and solar energy and windmills.

Again the invisible finger banking on our insecurities.

THE LATEST POINT ON D/S OF AGRICULTURAL PRODUCTS (May 22-2011)

Based on an interview from Geopolitis with the head director of the F.A.O. (U.N) on rising prices of food commodities are the same as stated before. To reiterate the reasons why food products are so high does not lie on one single factor. We mentioned that Russia is no more exporting grain, bad crops in Asia, big corporation buying big quantities, rising demand in general based on population growth and depleting world stock reserve, and corn being used to make ethanol in the US. The increased cost of fuel is another factor trickling down in all products, even crops.

I have to admit that the food crisis is real and world demand and supply are tight, but they have been tight in 2008 and some years before that.

The speculation aspect in the futures commodities market doesn't help at all by all means. Much money has been drawn into the commodities market since other investments were down since the financial crisis.

The second controllable factor is the use of corn to make ethanol accounts for 25% of the world crop. In a food crisis that seems to be a very bad move on the part of the US government to encourage this conversion and to even subsidize the industry. The result is a price increase on corn for the rest of the world. This is a finger by the US government.

The third culprit is that very limited investments were done in agriculture. I don't know if arable land is getting scarce but some countries are investing in other countries to buy arable land like South Korea through Daewood, which is purchasing land in Madagascar and Saudi Arabia as well since they are surrounded by sand. Since world inventory (stock) has been diminishing for the last ten years, the tightness is real.

In summary, if speculators, the corn used for fuel, and rising oil prices were not in the equation, we would have a reasonable rise in demand based on population growth and emerging markets only.

Not that the increase on cereals is done voluntarily, but accidentally by men.

All these three factors mentioned are induced by men's greed. Will science save us for being able to grow more, increasing the supply?

Not science yet but people are going green and raising locally, in New York city. New York Grange has been born to raise crops on top of buildings. If *this is not a sign that things are getting tight and people want more natural produce and at reasonable cost, I don't know what is.*

Way to go! New York Grange.

JUNE FIRST-SOME REAL WEATHER NEWS
AFFECTING CROPS.-CNN NEWS.

Droughts are behind some major exports of wheat slowdowns in France, the second largest exporter next to the US, a drop of shipment of 59%. Droughts are also present in China and the US. Will the increase of Russia's export and Ukraine and increased harvest from Morocco and Egypt will suffice to fill the gap?

One factor to consider is that countries have bought more than enough to create substantial storage during the month of January and February reacting to political unrest. ''It was panic buying,'' according to David Eudall, an analyst at the Home Grown Cereals Authority in England. ''The fundamentals were not there''

Russian will ban it stop on exports May 28 and they say that farmers managed to plant 10% more grain and is expecting a 15% increase in the harvest.

Demand in grains will decrease slightly from Egypt, Morocco, Tunisia, and Algeria will be unchanged. France's export is predicted to decline by 12% and other European countries as well.

The USDA reports that the US crops are in poor conditions since 1966.

Will the present stock suffice and the increase of Russia's export to damper demand without increasing prices once again?

So far this year, to date, the global food prices rose 36% according to United Nation's figures.

We had an unrealistic demand from chaos buying and now we will have limited supply cause by factual droughts and an increase in supply which was cut off previously by the first panic buying which will leave us in a quagmire for the rest of the year.

The French wheat futures rose 80% in the past twelve months. What is in the offing for speculators for the rest of the year?

CHAPTER FIVE-

ADVERTIZING/ LABELLING DECEPTIONS.

Organic foods VS Agricultural revolution.

All   products on the shelves are designed to be
attractive   to consumers including the information stated.

Adding slogan like; sugar free, reduced in salt by 50%, all
natural biological and all Green or new improved makes a
difference in customer's choice since people want better and
more natural products with less additives and preservatives.
The inevitable question arises: -is it true what they say on the
box?
If you see a picture of Grammas' on a jar, is it really a
Gramma which made it? Is it a Gramma own recipe? Is
''Home Made'' really comes from a home and not a factory?
It sounds trivial because down deep we know it is not true but
it is still a lie. A little white lie perhaps, but still not true but
present to give us assurance of quality.

The other section which seems over boarding with information
is the beauty products like shampoos, conditioners, gels,
sprays and lotions and potions. A lot are fruit based or herbal
based, all natural with cocoa and oats and buttery texture like
honey and milk.
All these products sound good, too good almost, good enough
to be eaten instead of putting it on your body or scalp.
For some reason, I don't see a ''fruit section'' where people
would be quizzing oranges and cutting apricots, pineapples
and watermelons to be put in beauty products eventually. It
would look more like a kitchen rather than a chemical factory.

The world of perfumes and cologne is quite a world of its own, putting products out there by very distinguish firms and star names and reputable brand names. In a recent study done by EWG.org on fragrance ingredients, they found that out of 17 products tested, there were 14 secret chemicals which could not be identified. They said that this is ''the secret'' which makes the difference and that nobody can copy.

We know that the fruit flavors are not natural nor comes from fresh fruits. They are essence of fruits, chemicals to resemble authentic smells. I'm sure that detergent companies with their lemon additive never purchased a lemon for the production.

So, where does that leave us? For the most part, there is a big unknown in what we consume and consumers want to go the natural way, shying away from unknown chemicals and their unknown effect on the body. We would like to understand what is written on the labels and have labels for everything including meat products, fish, chicken where the labelling laws are not required.

The Organic Consumer Association goes a long way to be active in labelling laws on all products and check to see if they are lies on products labelling or not the total truth.

We can handle the truth.

They feel that people should know if our foods have been modified genetically (GMO) or they are Frankenfoods or confined animal feeding operations (CAFO).

Monsanto Company is a large contributor to increase our food production so that the world won't starve but society is back peddling on chemical use in or on our foods.

From pesticides to fertilizers to hormone feeding, Monsanto is part of our kitchen or ''Monsanto Meals.''

From petitions to rally, to lawsuits, the OCA is present with thousands of mothers caring about what is going into their children's body. They want to know if what they eat has been genetically engineered (GE) or not and they are poisoning their children or not.

It is simply a basic right to information.

For example; to know if the milk you buy has (rBGH) in it, a bovine growth hormone which is transferred into the milk and which has been banned in several countries already.

Most European countries (27) and Canada have banned the use of this hormone and it is accepted in the U.S, the country where we can find the most cancer cases and where the cost of managing disease is the highest.

Fertilizers are part of the agricultural revolution where it increased the yields of crops and the use of land more often. Some will contradict these results (PAN.org) by saying that our food comes mostly from small farms and crops lost to insect are still higher that they were before.

And if we were serious about feeding the world, we wouldn't use corn to be put in our gas tanks.

Companies will undoubtedly deny that pesticides are dangerous and the argument saying that it depends on the amount of the dose. In small quantity is not dangerous. Since we have been eating unknown chemicals for many years, I guess they must be right on that point. I think we must be immune to all kinds of poisons by now.

Most people will trust the government to make sure companies don't literally poison us along the way. As I mentioned before, they are too many chemicals in this world to be tested and a big unknown about their effects on human beings in the long term.

Some will swear that pesticides and fertilizers are the cause of many children diseases and allergies. One has to look for oneself by knowing exactly what you eat.

The jury is still out on the harm of chemicals and companies will fight lawsuits after lawsuits and will take pride saying that their products are the answer to climate change and the world shortage of food.

We did experience a ''green revolution'' where our crop yields were increased considerably and made food more available to the billions of people (and still growing) but *World Hunger* is still around and not only in Africa but also in the US. What will happen in 2050 when the world population reaches 9 billion people?

The world hunger problem is not only of shortage of food but it is a question of poverty. If you can't buy the food, income is the problem, not food yields. That explains why there are kids starving in North America as well, in the land of plenty. Since we (US & Canada) export food, we have more than we need.

So, are genetically modified foods (GMO) or organisms really the answer?

Are we paying the price because we don't know yet if it is bad or good for us?

Dr. Philip Bereano from University of Washington did spend lots of time, three decades, studying the issue. In an interview with Dr. Mercola in his daily letter, safety issues were asked about GMO.

The most succinct answer is ''we don't know if it is safe because there is no arbitrary research'' said Dr. Bereano, ''only that the companies like Monsanto (biotech company) tell us it is safe.''

A paradox was established when the FDA announced the GMO foods were no different from ordinary foods and then, Monsanto Company had filed for patents arguing that their GM products are completely unique from their conventional counterparts and therefore must receive patent protection and monopoly.

The debate is not over and probably just starting since they are no evidence of benefits either.

In an economic approach, benefits have to be weighed against social cost. (Expensive GM seed-health-medical cost) Capability of feeding the world seems benefit enough to out weight any cost doesn't it?

But not according to *Agroecological* projects, where it can increase yields of crops, thus production.

In a publication produced by the UN, as recently as March 8, '*'Eco-farming can double Food production in ten years.*''

''To feed 9 billion people in 2050, we urgently need to adopt the most efficient farming techniques available'' says Olivier De Schutter, UN Special Reporter on the right to food and author of the report. Today's scientific evidence demonstrates that Agra-ecological methods outperform the use of chemical fertilizers in boosting food production where the hungry live-especially in unfavorable environments.''

''To date, agro-ecological projects have shown an average crop yield increase of 80% in 57 developing countries with an average increase of 116% in all Africa projects,'' De Schutter says....

This goes to the heart of the problem where you are ' *'using small farms* '' and ' *'located where it is needed.*'' Increasing yields on large industrial farms located in North America doesn't solve the problem of poverty and hunger. So, there is another route besides pesticides and fertilizers and one should know if we are eating Franken-chicken or naturally grain feed chicken!

The food industry always comes at us with little surprises that we usually find out the hard way by food poisoning or even death.

Using tricks to make us believe that what we are buying something else rather than what it is, is really not new but always more expensive. The latest is using *MEAT GLUE* to put low grade meats (with more fat) together as it appears to be one piece of quality meat and of course you would be

195

charged as it were high quality meat. The meat glue is an enzyme called *TRANSGLUTAMINASE*, come in powder form and produced by the Ajinomoto Co. the one which produces Aspartame.

They take small pieces of meat, the unwanted ones, put them in tightly in cellophane, sprinkle with glue powder and put it the fridge for a while. When you take it out, it is *one piece* of meat.

Personally, I don't much about beef since I rarely eat any (six times a year or so) so, one can fool me easily with different names of cuts and charge anything they want.

The danger of thinking that you have high quality and low fat meat might be a problem if you undercook it and swallow uncooked fats or fats that doesn't show or well hidden. If you cook it until it becomes a hockey puck, the risk is minimized. So, be on the lookout of meat glue.

Another trick is to pump water in a large piece of meat so that it weighs more. No danger in added water but your cost would be lower without it.

Another little *finger* from our butcher.

PACKAGING & LABELLING

Packaging and labelling is an industry of its own because it does encompass many topics to be revealed as ''information access'' of mass produced food.

''The objective of foodstuff labelling is to guarantee that consumers have access to complete information on the content and composition of products, in order to protect their health and their interest. Labelling of certain non-food products must also contain particular information, in order to guarantee their safe use and allow consumers to exercise real choices. In addition, the packaging of foodstuffs must adhere to production criteria in order to avoid contaminating food products.'' (Source: EUROPA. EU legislation/consumer).

It does cover a wide spectrum of legal points as; labelling, presentation and advertising.

It covers GM food and feed-traceability-novel foods and ingredients-nutrition-health claims-instant formulas-spreadable fats-edible caseins-aromatized drinks-products to improve the organoleptic properties-plastic materials- vinyl chloride monomer-ceramic-cellulose-animal testing-dangerous substance and so on.

One can see that a lot is being covered by regulations and verified by consumers' associations and consumers at large. These are the European regulations and I'm sure the FDA covers all these items as well.

I don't know if I should summarize all these aspects of regulation and labelling, or simply mentioned that consumers have a right and responsibility to read the information provided and ask for more information if needed particularly on meat products, where information is rather scarce. It is good to know what the animal ate while raising. Was it grains, seeds, grass corn and if hormones were used.

Here is a summary of compulsory labelling particulars from the Europa. EU. /legislation which is presented in a concise manner. I'm sure the FDA has the same, or close to the same legislation but their web site is presented differently.

What the consumer should expect on food products;

-Name under the product is sold
-List of ingredients
-Quantity of ingredients
-Net quantity
-Date of minimum durability
-Special storage condition of use
-Name of business
-Place of origin
-Instruction for use
-Acquired alcoholic strength
-Safety safeguard clause

-Other language labelling

One can see that there is a lot of information required but of course that doesn't include meats and fresh vegetables and fruits except for the date of minimum durability for meat. (Expired date of use) Fresh vegetables and fruits have revealed lots of information just by looking at it. It would be redundant to put provenance and instructions and safety measures.

Consumer's expectation for pre-packed products;

-Weight and volume based on the minimum and maximum requirements.

Consumer's expectations on price offered;

Identification of prepared foodstuff by lot;

Food stuff treated with ionizing radiation;

-The conditions for authorization for radiation

-Sources of ionized radiation

-Dosimetry of ionized radiation

Quick frozen foods;

-Must say on the label quick frozen

-Must not vary between 3d.c or a maximum of 6d.c depending where it is shipped.

For quality associated with the origin, processing or production method.

Agricultural products and foodstuff as traditional specialities guaranteed (TSG)

-Application must be made to receive the TSG status and approved by a commission.

Protection of Geographical Indications and designation of Origin.

-Must be registered by either origin (PGO) or by identification (PGI)

Production and labelling of organic products;

-It covers organic farming for plants, animals and fish

Debate on the eco-labelling of fisheries products;

Not much has been done on this issue and debates are still going on.

GMO-genetically modified organism;

Must be labelled as such with also foodstuff that contains traces by adventitious of GMO

Novel Foods;

Novel food should be labelled as to mention composition-nutritional value or intended use

-Divulged presence of materials that might have implications

-Divulged materials which give rise to ethical concerns

Nutrition and Allergens labelling;

As to be clearly stated for consumers to understand and vitamins added and minerals directly mentioned on food stuff.

Coffee and Chicory and Quinine;

Have to mention if it is extracted or soluble or instant.

Infant formulae and process food and cereal for children;

The specific content of vitamins and or minerals if infant are not breastfeed.

Foodstuffs for particular nutritional uses;

Must include composition or manufacturing process, energy value and carbohydrates, fat content per 100grams.

Foodstuff used in energy-restricted diets for weight reduction;

Must include specific directives.

Dietary foods for special medical purposes;

Must include complete formula.

Meats: Beef and Veal;

The specification is quite elaborate and detailed. It must show registration of cattle for identification and provenance. Individual cattle passport if imported and mincemeat must identify provenance or link with animal. See site for full labelling and registration regulations.

Oils and fats & Blends and levels of Erucic Acid;

Oils and fats for human consumption of > than 5% and < than 90% by weight.

Identification if it is dairy or non-dairy or vegetable fats.

Milk Derivatives;
Partly or wholly dehydrated preserved milk should be mentioned.
Must include authorized additives, nutrition, and labelling for infant formulas. Must mention additional of vitamins, minerals and supplement foodstuff.
Edible caseins and caseinates;
They are the proteins found in milk. Authorized enzymes must be mentioned.
Beverages;
Natural Mineral waters must mentioned place of origin, contents of minerals, the treatment used and potability. Must have been submitted to separation of iron, manganese and sulfur and arsenic by the treatment of ozone. Must not have any effect from touch, taste and smell and must be packaged at all times to prevent contamination.
Fruits juices and similar products have to mention if mixed with other blend juices, or concentrate and if sugar added.
Aromatized drinks
Labelling of alcoholic beverages as % per volume
Sugars and Honey;
There are 11 types of sugars that should be clearly identified. White sugar-semi-white sugar-extra white sugar-sugar solution-invert sugar solution-invert sugar syrup-glucose syrup-dried glucose syrup-dextrose-dextrose anhydrous-fructose.
Fruits jams and sweetened chestnut purée; % of sugar included.
Cocoa and chocolate. % of power of cocoa, milk etc.
Honey. Its origin.
Products added to improve the organoleptic properties of foods;
Authorization procedures for:
Food additives;

There is a list of additives which are deemed to be acceptable for human consumption;
Food flavourings;
Authorized flavoring only;
Food enzymes;
The type of enzyme should be mentioned and be on the approved list.
Extraction solvents used in foodstuff;
Must be known product and approved and mention of provenance, batch number etc.
Note: All foods authorized products are for harmonization and consumer safety and consumer information. Much detailed information is available on; (Europa. EU/Legislation_Summary/consumer.)

As stated before, many of these regulations and legislation hopefully are similar or equal to the FDA in the US and in Canada. They are not 100% equal since some chemicals for instance have been banded for use or consumption in Europe and have *not* been banded in the United States. I am sure that the FDA has an opinion on all these products but the conclusion might differ like it does with certain chemicals and proteins use as we mentioned earlier on
(rBGH)

FOOD PAKAGING AND CONTAINERS

Active and intelligent packaging is submitted for approval of many (17) materials that comes in contact with food. Producing companies should have quality control mechanisms to protect food against all packaging products and have approval of such. Verification of potential mutagenic, carcinogenic, toxic material is subject to authorization.

PLASTICS

By in large, using this form of packaging is highly regulated and must comply with rigorous standards.
Plastic materials and articles;
Recycling plastic materials and articles;
Testing migration of plastic;
Testing of materials in contact with foodstuffs;
Restrictions of Oxy derivatives in food packaging;
Materials and articles containing vinyl chloride monomer;
Release of N-nitrosamines from rubber teats;
CERAMICS
Must declare limits of lead and cadmium in ceramics which comes in contact with food.
CELLULOSE
Material and articles in regenerating cellulose film;
Under specific direct regulations
NON-FOOD PRODUCTS LABELLING
Ecolabel;
Product energy consumption;
Description & Tests
Energy efficiency of office equipment;
The Energy Star program (EU & US)
Ecodesign for energy-using appliances;
Household appliances; energy consumption labelling;
In order to reduce the environmental impact.
Naming and labelling textile products;
Name and composition.
Labelling of footwear;
Mentioning the two main compositions of the article.
Cosmetic products: composition, labelling, animal testing;
Detergents;
Information on the fuel consumption and CO_2 emission on new cars;

Classification, packaging and labelling, of chemicals and their mixture;
Of dangerous substances;
Of dangerous preparations;

To obtain more detailed information, go on site: Europa.
EU/legislation_summary/

I THOUGHT I WAS GETTING BIGGER

Have you noticed that even if some of the prices are stable, containers are getting smaller?
It is evident with cereal boxes and beers bottles or cans like Heineken for instance and Coke bottles. They are ''kinda'' cute though. Here is short list where it might be more difficult to notice:
Tropicana orange juice went from 64 oz. to 59 oz.
Ivory dish detergent from 30oz to 24 oz.
Kraft single cheese from 24 slices to 22
Chicken by the Sea salmon from 3.0 oz. to 2.6 oz.
One pound of coffee now ¾ of a pound for the same price
And I'm sure they are others since it's less conspicuous to alter the package rather than raising prices. Nevertheless, it still inflation and one have to do the math on every product to find the real price increase. Since most people won't even notice the change, I find these at bit conniving. The *finger again* to consumers by big Corporations.

CHAPTER SIX-

FINANCIAL DECEPTIONS-FUND FONDLING

WHITE COLLAR CRIMES
THE INFAMOUS PONZI SCHEME

Mentioned earlier of the notorious schemes of financial advisers, Bernard Madoff and the likes, the Ponzi scheme came from a famous named based on the original Charles Ponzi, who voluntary paid good returns on early investments with new money from other later clients coming in.
Simple enough to understand and probably easier to do today than it was in the good old days, where computers can do just about anything, forging documents, making logos, looking like authentic statements.
Charles Ponzi did finish in jail and broke. Makes you wonder why people are so obstinate of following in his tracks and do end up in jail as well. Not that I don't understand wanting the big life, but most of them, like Bernard Madoff and many others who got caught afterwards doing the same thing, we're not living in poverty before they decided to astray of a life of crime.
They all had contacts with rich people, could talk with a ''silver tongue'' and smart enough to lie constantly and of course being very persuasive.

Charles Ponzi was born in 1882 in Lugo Italy and who himself was inspired by William F. Miller, a Brooklyn bookkeeper. Everybody needs a mentor.
After arriving in Boston in 1903 after university attendance in Rome, he worked in a restaurant as a dishwasher and learned English. He moved to Montreal where he worked for Banco

Zarosi and stayed with him until his bank failed and Zarosi fled to Mexico.

Charles Ponzi was penniless and was caught stealing money from a bank's client by forging a check. He spent three years in the St-Vincent de Paul prison.

He moved to the States and was caught helping illegal immigrants getting into the country and was convicted for two years in Atlanta prison.

After prison he married and worked odd jobs with his father in law until he received an international coupon reply from a company in Spain (IRC) asking about a catalogue. He investigated the coupon and the IRC could be bought in Italy and redeemed in the US for a much higher price. In other words, there was easy money to be made in the spread. The IRC was a way to exchange currency without really buying the currency and profit from the exchange (arbitrage) difference. He went on to a bigger scale, created a company and employed agents to sell the idea with hefty commissions and became richer by embarking people promising some 50% return in just a few months. He bought The Hanover Trust Bank of Boston after making millions. It worked until his scheme didn't work anymore and had to cover returns with new investor's money. He was living high on the hog and began to raise suspicion among financial people. Under investigation, his scheme to pay Peter with Paul's money became public and people made a run on his company to cash their money.

Charles Ponzi ended up to be convicted (86 counts of mail fraud) and sent to prison.

After many ''in'' and ''out'' of prison, he ended up at the State prison in Massachusetts for seven years. When he got out he was caught selling swampland in Florida where he ended up in a Florida State prison. He was deported back to Italy since he never became a US citizen and tried hopelessly different tricks and ended up in Brazil working for an airline company and being a translator.

His health became fragile, had a heart attack and became blind. He died on January 1949 totally broke in a Rio de Janeiro hospital. (See Wikipedia Encyclopedia for full story)

Nobody learns their lessons, that crooks get caught eventually because all things run its course- Even the good ones and certainly the bad ones.

It is not my high standard of morale that makes me wonder why these people do that, telling them that it's wrong to steal and dictating; ''shame on you.'' My sanctimonious conscience doesn't run that high because I know that it is tempting when the opportunities arise. The part that amazes me is that these ''crooks'' are rich to begin with and only want more on the hides of others. They are willing to spend people's life savings to buy a Van Gogh or a new Roll Royce. That, what burns me up; victimizing people who have done no wrong besides giving trust.

I'm sure Madoff was earning a good living before he decided to live a crook's life. Conrad Black had many castles around the globe before stealing his shareholders for just a few paltry millions more. Martha Stewart, the billionaires, went to jail for wrong doing in some public investments using inside information and lying to the courts.

Many more money managers were caught doing the old ''Ponzi scheme'' again and again, thinking there was an art to it, perfecting it and would never get caught.

The executives of Enron, Tyco and Lehman Brothers were not exactly poor before they cheated on ordinary people's hide.

If I was living in a small mansion, driving a fancy car(s) and sitting on a good wine cellar, I would be thinking how I can have more. One can only eat three times a day, right? And of course, the trillion dollar bailout of Wall Street when, in the same year of receiving public money, the executives enhanced their income by giving themselves bonuses, a reward for legally screwing the Government, thus, the people; - again. Far from being Jean Val Jean (Victor Hugo) who stole one piece of bread because he was hungry, isn't it?

One wonders if business attracts crooks and villains, but they always have been everywhere, in all kinds of business. In the later cases of Enron executives and the others, I don't think they were dishonest to begin with but turn out to be disloyal given the opportunity. That doesn't extinguish the problems of falsifications and embezzlements. We have to refine the framework of surveillance by the authorities. There are always going to be unscrupulous opportunists to con easy money.

JULY 21-2011-BLOOMBERG NEWS

Another one bites the dust.

Danielle Chiesi, former New Castle Funds LLC analyst was convicted to 2 1/2 years in jail for passing tips to Galleon Group LLC.

Quite a long time for a few minute phone call. I'm sure the judge wanted to give a real strong message to Wall Street about miss using insider's information.

JULY 23-2011-NO END TO GRREDY PEOPLE

K 1 Hedge Fund Group's Helmut Kiener was found guilty of defrauding clients with a Ponzi scheme with investors' money for the amount $497 million. He was sentenced to 10 years and 8 months for fraud. It is quite a high price to pay for only buying and driving a Roll Royce and other fancy cars around the bloc. As much as I like Ferraris and Lamborghinis, a little sportier than a RR, I wouldn't be tempted to steal someone else's money to drive one. The pleasure of owning one of these ''little beauties'' his to feel that you have reached success on your own terms and efforts: not stealing it. I'm sure he was already making a nice living being a fund manager. Will they ever learn?

WHY DO WE HATE INSURANCE COMPANIES SO MUCH?

Insurance companies are firms which people love to hate. We are more or less obligated to buy insurances (car-house-life) and in most cases, we pay premiums for nothing because the majority doesn't make claims, otherwise, they wouldn't make money if the majority would make claims and collect. Of course everybody dies and the bereaved family can console themselves with a few extra bucks. But insurance companies are unscrupulous enough to forgo payment when the time is due. I've read that companies pay only 50% of the claims and the other 50% are not eligible because of fault on the part of the policy holder. Either there was undeclared sickness, or the death didn't qualify as an accident or there was something in the fine print, a condition that permits the insurance company to withhold payment.

Since ordinary people are overwhelmed at the time by grief and often oppressed by large companies, they can't really concentrate on legal matters and are penniless to be able to fight legally what should be due payment.

In the recent case of Jane Pierce (Montana) which had to sue the insurance company when her husband died in a car accident. The company (MetLife) said it was a suicide and not an accident. End of story.

Source: Bloomberg News March first 2011.

How can a company make such a statement when knowing the husband had fought cancer for years and was a family man? She finally won after a legal battle with no extra compensation of interest on the $224,000 she received. No more, no less.

It seems that insurance companies have a greater chance of not going to court since most people don't sued which have become part of their procedure or tactics to refrain from paying.

This is why most lawyers cherish cases involving insurance companies like it was picking daisies in an open field. This is also why people don't respect multi-million dollar insurance companies when they see they are trying (and succeed and sometimes in an obligation to pay) to screw individuals. These actions are done all the time and the *finger* is given to us all the time.

JULY 07-2011

Florida Insurance commissioner Kevin McCarty subpoena both MetLife and Prudential Financial Inc. for withholding payment of unpaid benefits to claimers for the amount of $1 Billion. (Source: Bloomberg News)

It is appalling to say the least, to see big corps screwing their own clients by holding back their dues.

If this not a *finger to consumers* by the sheer bigness of multinationals, I don't know what is.

HEADQUARTERS OFFSHORE.

Most people despise paying taxes because it always seems too much for what they get in return but Corporations do hate it as much. With tax experts, the CEO is the first to escape taxes as much as possible in order to enhance shareholder benefits. If the shareholders are happy, the CEO gets to keep his job. Transferring headquarters to tax heaven is not new since they are well known places like the Bahamas, Grand Cayman, Switzerland and others who do not collect taxes from corporations establish there neither from individuals on their personal income. Taxes on goods and services, which are high, suffice to local governments. Both the Bahamas and Grand Cayman are small islands in tropical weather and require very little infrastructure and are not expanding. Switzerland is also a small country and very well known for its secretive banking and low tax rate.

Corporate tax is 15% which is half of the US which is at 35%. The Canadian corporate tax rate is 18% but personal income tax runs as high as 48%.

The US government gave a good effort of trying to stop US companies from moving their headquarters in the island but had very little success with Switzerland. Perhaps it is their conscience that corporations are willing to pay 15% of net profits as opposes to zero in the islands.

It is surprising to see that big US corporations operating in the US, which have most of their personnel working in the US, have their administration in the US with their executives residing in the US have a headquarters in Switzerland. We are talking about companies like Google, Cisco, General Electric and other major international companies in the oil exploration-services have headquarters in Switzerland. The pharmaceutical industry is well known to have headquarters in Switzerland and receives other benefits like subsidized studies and easily accepted clinical trials.

Companies play cat and mouse with their taxes as much as individuals do, except the amount owed totals in the billions. With the US government deficit being in the limelight these days, it just seems unfair that companies don't pay their full share by simply moving some documents into another country with little personnel or just a mailbox number.

At the end, it is the individual that pays by an increase of income taxes in order to balance the books. We see now many countries going under like New Zealand, Portugal, Spain, and Greece which have to be bailed out by other countries like Germany and the IMF.

Everybody has to be accountable for their actions, even governments.

I find it appalling, when governments can't meet their payroll or payments on their debt. Sure, governments don't go away, they have unlimited life as oppose to people, but still I wonder why excess spending occurs on all levels. I guess this is a subject for another book.

Some major corporations are able to cook the books even if they are profitable. Writing off expenses allowed getting back funds from the IRS and avoiding a major part of taxes due.

Exxon Mobil

Exxon Mobil made $19 billion in profits in 2009. Exxon not only paid no income tax, it actually received a $156 million rebate from the IRS, according to its SEC filings.

Bank of America

Bank of America received a $1.9 billion tax refund from the IRS last year, although it made $4.4 billion in profits and received a bailout from the Federal Reserve and the Treasury Department of nearly $1 trillion.

General Electric

Over the past five years, while General Electric made $26 billion in profits in the United States, it received a $4.1 billion refund from the IRS.

Chevron

Chevron received a $19 million refund from the IRS last year after it made $10 billion in profits in 2009.

Boeing

Boeing, which received $30 billion contract from the Pentagon to build 179 airborne tankers, got a $124 million refund from the IRS last year.

Citigroup

Citigroup last year made more than $4 billion in profits but paid no federal income tax. It received a $2.5 trillion bailout from the Federal Reserve and the US Treasury.

Goldman Sachs

Goldman Sachs in 2008 only paid 1.1 percent of its income in taxes even though it earned profits of $2.3 billion and received an almost $800 billion from the Federal Reserve and the US Treasury Department.

ConocoPhillips

ConocoPhillips, the fifth largest oil company in the United States, made $16 billion in profits in 2007 through 2009, but received $451 million in tax break through the oil and gas manufacturing deduction.

Carnaval

Over in the past five years, Carnaval Cruise Lines made more than $11 billion in profits, but its federal income tax rate during those years was just 1.1 percent.

Source: Wealth Wire-Worst corporate Income tax avoiders

These billions of missing tax payment go directly at the government deficit which in turn will be paid by contributors eventually. It is another finger at us, ''the people'' by the adamant boldness of corporations.

Today, July 8 2011, another company joins the tax evader group; Caterpillar Inc.

One of the its ex-employee, Daniel J. Schlicksup, the global tax strategist for the company from 2005 to 2008 is suing the company because now, he is out of a job and was demoted for squealing against the firm.

He explained how Caterpillar was using one of their subsidiaries to sell merchandise, mainly parts over the world from its Switzerland branch and escaping US taxes which should have been paid because it was only a book entry, since their parts warehoused are in the US.

There is no activity in the abroad branch, no personnel and certainly no parts which his by the way, the most lucrative segment of the company.

Now the US government wants to raise taxes and cut social security.

This $ 2 billion tax dodge would come handy right now.

The little guy takes it on the chin again; the *finger* by big corporations.

INSIDE INFORMATION

Inside information is the most common phrase in the security's market like candy is to kids. It is done all the time by brokers, traders, and clients. Everyone knows someone on the inside of a public company and those just can't keep the lid on positive information before it gets legally published. It has been done for years and it will continue for years to come.

Even former NASDAQ director got caught with his hands in the cookie jar trading on inside information on behalf of his wife's account from his own personal computer. (May 31-2011)

Donald Johnson pleaded guilty to the US department of Justice and he's liable to go to prison for it for 20 years. He pocketed $640,000 for his illegal trading.

It seems to me that the amount is not large enough to go to prison for because it comes out to $32,000 a year. I'm sure he earned much more than that with his job.

The point being is that many uses inside information and get away with it since they are thousands of trades per minutes and it is impossible to verify all of them. Inside information is like ''Ecstasy,'' just too good to resist.

One thing good about it is that regulators scratches their head to implement new guidelines and ''blockers'' to illicit trading. Even bank regulations and minimum deposits and margins are questioned to limit the ease of too much risky liquidity without a fundamental secured base.

HIGH-FREQUENCY TRADING

High-frequency trading is not new but recent. It must be a child of automatic trading when fund manager uses by putting automatic ''limit buy orders'' and ''limit sell orders'' at a certain price.

The computer did the work. Now HFT is done with gigantic computers and buy and sell stocks at a penny profit and it's been done thousands of times a minute. It's done by algorithmic process and executed in a fraction of a second thousands of times.

It is as far as you can get from fundamental trading and surpassing technical trading.

So much of value in the stock market! It is the biggest casino in the world.

The pro and cons of it might be argued because it does bring closer the BID & ASK, thus providing liquidity. Approved by the SEC in 1998, HFT is growing and will grow into other markets as in currencies and commodities. By 2010 HFT accounted for over 70% of equity trades taking place in the US and was rapidly growing in popularity in Europe and in Asia. (Source: Wikipedia)

Most high-frequency trading strategies fall within one of four groups of trading strategies;

-Market making
-Ticker tape trading
-Event arbitrage
-H.F Statistical Arbitrage

The magic of HFT is that information about a price of a stock is known before ordinary broker or banks computers showing the info on their screens; only a few seconds but enough time to make some trades. There are many companies in this type of trading which are willing to spend millions on fast computer services. It seems like they could make billions but my point is that, it does confirm my saying that there is no fundamental value in the stock market.

It does seem like calculating ratios of a company and evaluating management is a thing of the past.

Texas Fund Manager Convicted by Jury in ''Life Settlement'' Insurance Scheme.
Published Bloomberg on June 11-2011.

And I thought we were done with ''white collar crime'' for a while.

''Adley H. Abdulwahad, one of the principals at Houston-based A&O Resources Management Ltd. charged with stealing $103 million in a death benefits scheme, was found guilty by a federal court in Virginia of conspiracy, securities fraud and money laundering, prosecutors said. The investment involved life insurance policies that were sold to a third party, with the policy owner getting a cash payout while the buyer of the settlement investment paid the premium to maintain the policy and collect the benefit upon the death of the insured person, prosecutors said in September when Abduwalad was charged.''

Abduwalad, 35, and his colleagues stole money from 800 people across the US and Canada, including elderly retirees who lost their life savings, in a scheme to sell'' life settlements''
said U.S. attorney Neil MacBride.

When a BMW doesn't suffice, steal money from retirees to get a Ferrari.

As much as I love Ferraris, I don't think I would enjoy it much in prison.

SHARDS OF THE FINACIAL MELTDOWN ARE STILL HOT AS GOVERNMENT INVESTIGATORS PROBE INTO FORECLOSURE CONDUCT OF **BANK OF AMERICA**.
(June 14-2011) (Source: Bloomberg news)

''The bank was slow in providing data and offered incomplete information, according to the US Department of Housing and Urban Development (HUD) inspector general's office, which conducted the review.''

When I spoke of the power struggle between government and corporations, this is a perfect example of how large institutions are pulling against each other for transparency.

''Submitted as an exhibit in a lawsuit by the State of Arizona against the Charlotte, North Carolina-based bank., in Arizona, which is seeking to interview former Bank of America employees , accused the bank of misleading homeowners who were seeking mortgage modifications.''

One reason all this paper work his incomplete and sometimes forged, it is that, all these mortgage loans were insured by the government. Now, BAC is filling for loan default to the government for a total of $5.7 billion through 40,219 claims. This is addition to the $46 billion the lender booed so far and expecting an additional $27 billion between now and 2013.

''One issue is whether loan documents were properly transferred to the Trust. The Trust issued securities to investors backed by the pools of mortgage loans. A second issue is the due diligence performed on the quality of the loans going into the Trust and the representations made to investors.''

As I mentioned before, the rating of Standard & Poor's were AAA or AA+ on these financial instruments that were impossible to evaluate. It was rated on a theoretical basis only not physically examining the documents because they were simply too many. Since mortgage loans are backed by brick and mortar, they should be safe. In all practical purposes, the brick and mortar doesn't have anything to do with the loan only that it is collateral serving as a guarantee against to loan. The ability to pay is the real factor, not the collateral. What does the collateral mean when markets are sinking?

It is like giving a ''submarine'' as collateral. Who needs a submarine?

The main features of these loans were the fact that they were insured by the government (FHA). If anything goes wrong, just file for reimbursement. That is why ''high rating'' was issued.

Other financial institutions are under investigation as well like Deutsche Bank for instance and Wells Fargo and JP Morgan Chase & Co.

FIGHTING ON BOTH FRONTS

If facing enemies with guns and bombs is not enough, how about repossessing your house back home while you're fighting for your life? And find out that your kids are living in a motel?

Sounds too cruel!!

JP Morgan Chase &Co. just fire an executive, David Lowman, mortgage chief, for overcharging active-duty military personnel on loans and improperly foreclosed on their borrowers.

First, these loans are protected by the Service Members Act, which protects these loans against default.

Second, who with a sane mind would act against a military fighting overseas by putting his wife and children on the streets?

''In April, JP Morgan agreed to pay $56 million and to reduce mortgage rates for all deployed soldiers to settle claims that it overcharged military personnel on their mortgages and seized homes of 27 duty military personnel who were protected by the Service Members Act.''

''We're sorry.'' Said one company spokesman at the annual shareholder's meeting.

Really? Sorry doesn't cut it.

''Bank of America, the largest U.S lender, and JP Morgan
Stanley's Saxon Mortgage Services Inc. also paid millions of
dollars to settle similar lawsuits with military personnel. Bank
of America agreed last month to pay $20 million to settle a
lawsuit alleging improper foreclosure on about 160 members
of the military between January 2006 and May 2009, the
Justice Department said in a May 26 statement. New York
bases Morgan Stanley also agreed to pay $2.35 million to
resolve a lawsuit alleging it an improper foreclosure on 17
service members between January 2006 to June 2009.''
''Cindy Amine was hired to oversee a separate consent
agreement that JPM and 13 other banks reached with the
Office of the Controller of the Currency (OCC) and the
Federal Reserve in April over foreclosure practices.''
When someone wrote; Too big to fail.- He or she forgot to
add; Too big to fail to screw us.
The invisible finger again.

Boiler rooms are still popular since Zvi Goffer and his brother,
Emanuel from Gallon Group LLC hedge fund manager,
pleaded guilty recently and the old *Boiler Room trick* is still
going strong. Baldwin Anderson, a salesman from Gryphon
Holdings Inc. pleaded guilty of misleading investors and
defrauding them of $ 20 million after Gryphon president
pleaded guilty. They even said that their office was in the
Exchange Tower on Wall Street while it was in a strip mall in
Staten Island.
Anderson was paid $1.1 million for his work.
Boys! It's been done before! They even made a movie about it
named '' The boiler room.''
Going from trading stocks to trading cigarette in prison. How!
One has to come up with a new trick.
JP Morgan is making the news again (June 16-2011) in
regards to ''credit protection missing payment insurance.''
The charge by the OCC is that this insurance policy for the

purchase of cars was sold under pressure and over charged to clients.

JP Morgan had to pay a fine of $2 million and reimbursed client of $25 million.

In order to look good and acting as a good citizen, JPM transferred top executives to another post.

JPM is too big since it bullied costumers.

It never seems to amaze me how big corporations deliberately screw the little guy.

Another finger at consumers.

TOP DOGS STEALING AGAIN

Credit Suisse's broker Eric Butler managed to postpone fraud conviction one more time but prison awaits.

Citigroup's vice president Gary Foster, 35 got arrested coming from vacation from Bangkok for embezzling 19 million from the bank by just transferring funds into his account. Sound too easy? Yes it is and it is easy to get caught as well.

One can have lots of fun with extra money, but you don't need lots of money to have fun in Bangkok. I think with a VP's salary you can wing it easily in that town, having two massages a day and some take ''home companionship'' for below 30 bucks. You couldn't even spend thousands of dollars on a conduct of turpitude even if you tried.

Mr. Foster should have gone to Bangkok before he stole some money, then he would have realized that it doesn't take much in the ''land of sin'' to have fun. I hope he has a good memory to reminisce in his souvenirs while in prison.

With a six figure income and some perks, I think I can have both ends meet.

THE BIG DOG WAS SLEEPING.-July 8th. 2011

Someone did literally shake the dog's house and said; time to wake up and bark.

The commissioner, Mr. Bart Chilton from Commodities Future Trading Commission (CFTC) is getting more power and hopefully more personnel to oversee trades, frauds, speculation and other misappropriated conduct in this market, where the population consensus is that speculation is the culprit of high oil price and high food prices.

He clearly admitted that there is a price component in each underlying commodity due to speculation. The amount is of course hard to tell since there are thousands of trades a day coming from all over. His estimate was perhaps .50 cents a gallon on retail price of gas.

Using that number even if it is an estimate, I think it is enough to have people choke on other spending and slow down the recovery. If Obama and Bernanke's release some oil from EIA strategic reserves, it is because they realized too late that the high gas price was enough to curtail other spending which would have occurred instead. It is a consumer driven economy, don't forget.

I really think if private speculators were not in the future commodity's market, the ones that are not users and producers of these commodities, prices would have been a lot more stable.

The young and hip commissioner seems to be going in the right direction, changing the law to give his Commission more access and transparency to this cobweb of financial products.

The other good news is that the present US Government is making Wall Street Reform by tightening the laws of banking, commercial and investment banking by appointing a new watchdog for the surveillance of these new laws. The

221

Government is also fed up of the power of banks toward the community and its influence towards the Government and its speculation on derivatives and creating new products to take savings away from investors.

Banks have two modes of operation. Being *conservative* when it comes to lending money to individuals or small companies and *speculative* with deposit money trying to make substantial profits.

Leon Kordzian, a real estate agent in Montreal was found guilty of stealing $868,000 from investors who subscribe to his recommendations of promising high return on their investments.

People will never learn to trust naively so called, ''know it all'' or a wizard money maker.

Investors didn't get a run for their money since he was convicted to ''home stay'' for his crime. It gives him time to count his money and dream what he is going to do with it.

I say poor judgment on the part of the Judge.

CHAPTER SEVEN-

GOVERNMENTAL DECEPTIONS.

FINANCIAL BAILOUTS OF COUNTRIES

In a public statement this week (March second 2011) Bernard Madoff himself said; ''that the US Government actions in the financial crisis is a Ponzi scheme.''
He accused some of the high officials of the SEC that help him steal millions from clients who were not convicted of any wrong doing or any bank executives.
It takes one to know one.
Since he was convicted to 115 years in jail, I'm sure he wants company.
The National Inflation Association says in writing that the US Government spending while saving US banks out of bankruptcy and the automobile industry will create hyperinflation in the system and major basic food hikes is expected in 2011. They say; (NIA) it is the worst move a Government has made.
We will see at the end of this year how things are. Now, sad thing to mention is that all that money didn't create jobs. Unemployment is still very high at 9%.
One thing politicians are worried about is the US government deficit which reaches in the trillions of dollars. By printing money seems the only way out since the US dollar can't be devalued because everything is labelled in US dollars.

Devaluations of currencies are done when the debt is too large to pay back, thus resettling the debt by the amount of the devaluation.

It was done in Germany in 1923, in Mexico in 1994, in Russia in 1998 and Argentina in 2002 and Turkey and Romania in 2005.

I don't mean to take this lightly but isn't just a ''Book adjustment'' with the World Bank and International Monetary Fund? Just resetting the dial and lets go, one more round of spending.

I know that currency is just fiat paper, but it seems that every big organization is running a deficit, borrowing either from the public or the neighbors or central banks and the IMF. The US dollar has not been backed by gold since 1971 and it is a floating and sinking dollar against most other currencies.

So, legally, you can't tender your dollar bill to the central bank because you will only get a newer bill and that's it.

If one thinks about it, you have Universities running a deficit, most cities borrow in the form of Municipal Bonds, States are running deficits so as Provinces in Canada and both Federal Governments are running a deficit and all countries in Europe since Portugal, Greece and Spain are in dire straits and most recently, New Zealand was bailed out by Germany.

And let's not forget the personal debt or household credit to banks by credit cards.

HOW! That is a lot of debt.

It seems like everything, the currency system is built on a house of cards and will collapse eventually. What is in the offing? A devalued US dollar or hyperinflation? (Which are the same by the way), - the enemy number one to all Central Banks.

The only good thing is that governments live forever, not like individuals, so they can pay back debt with new debt and so on at perpetuity. In other words, it is a Ponzi scheme since it is paying maturing debt by new debt. As long as the cost of these new debts is lower than the previous debt, everything is fine at the bottom line.

The only country experiencing real growth is China which finances the US by buying their treasury bonds like Japan did in the seventies. At this rate, China will own the world by 2035.
I will try to make sense of it all and keep a watchful eye on deficits and bail outs by the IMF, (which will run out of cash eventually,) to see how we are going to get out of that one.

But as most laymen would say; '' they only have to print more money, that's all.''
And in fact, that's what it sums up to since the US economy can't devalue its currency since it is the ''world currency''.
It's not like someone is going to send the bailiff over to seize government assets.
As a matter of fact, the government is able to borrow at 0.68% lower for a two year note, much lower than the 5.1% it did in 2007.
Tax revenues, as a percentage of the economy his at a 60 year low even if the Federal debt against economic output increased of 50%.
People or should I say, countries and banks are willing to lend (buy bonds) to the US Government since the insurance cost of $10 million note is $45, 830 compared with Argentina which is $665,000 for the same amount.
The cost of ten year bonds is 3.5% when it was 5.4% in 1990.
''Even if debt exceed income, it doesn't mean we are broke.''
Said John Boehner, House speaker in a public speech published in Bloomberg news, March 6-2011.
The trillions scare most people and especially the Republicans near election time. To most commoners, trillion is a number you can't even write down on paper. How many zeros again?

The Public debt which stands at $9.6 trillion represent only 63% of GDP, where in other countries, the debt are at 126.7%, 121%, 116% of GDP, for Greece, Japan, and Italy respectively.
Total Debt reaches $14.26 trillion in the U.S. which is 97.0% of GDP. **(Public of $9.6 + $4.6 intra-governmental debt)** The tax claims represent 24% of GPD when Denmark represents 48% of GDP.
So, the US government could raise taxes to get rid of the large chunk of the deficit.
Some say that intergovernmental debt shouldn't be considered since it is interest paid to the government. Intra-governmental debts are funds reserved for social programs.

BERNANKE'S CRITICS OF U.S. MONETARY POLICY

The financial or mortgage crisis of 2008-09 in the U.S was unprecedented in terms of a quick turnaround to a credit crunch in the economy which took down the world into a severe recession. That might be the reason why the US government or Bernanke's Federal Reserve Chairman and President Obama were propelled into uncharted waters. One didn't seem to have any choice of bailing banks and auto makers with billions of dollars when looking at the dismal possibilities of what might of happen without it. Nobody really stood up to say that was the wrong thing to do when the economy was on the verge of sinking. Only a few spoke after the fact but of course it was too late and nobody really knew the effects in the long run.

One simple equation which stands to reason is the fact that if you plow billions into an economy, inflation will show its ugly head very soon. Inflation is the enemy number one for all economies because there is only one tool to control it and it is by raising interest rates and taking the chance of choking the growth of the economy; - a tough balancing act.

Now in the first quarter of 2011, the bailouts seem to be working, slowly, but not without critics who are warning us of hyperinflation is coming soon, very soon.

When we can't blame ourselves about bad economic news forthcoming we can always blame China. China's growth frightens everybody even if the U.S. is running a balance of trade deficit. Jealously looking at their annual growth of just below 10% and declared inflation at 4.9%, China is not a threat to the US at those numbers. The only thing is that China did finance the U.S by buying U.S Treasury bonds, keeping their currency artificially low in relation to the dollar. By the same token, the US doesn't want s strong Yuan which might become the world reserve currency. The monetizing of the U.S debt or the massive bailout did force China to print money and spending it to support the dollar, keeping it low, have created inflation in their own country for the Chinese people. Some say that China's inflation rate is more like 10% as opposed to 4.9% reported.

The Q.E 1 and Q.E 2 and possibly Q.E.3 (quantitative easing) a new word for ''printing'' will put the U.S and the zero interest rate Federal Funds, into hyperinflation mode.
<u>Source: National Inflation Association</u>

Personally, I could see the erosion of the dollar by inflation if the billions of dollars printed went to the consumers, thus creating more spending and pushing prices upward. All these money exchanges between countries and the Treasury and Federal Reserve are somewhat mind boggling.

Someone's got to pay the piper eventually! Ready for a McDumpling?

THE FEDERAL RESERVE & US TRESURY EXPLAINED

The Treasury Department and the Federal Reserve are in cahoots in Treasury Bonds buying and selling which you wonder who is doing what to whom and where is it all going? I've looked up the description of their respective tasks and responsibilities and definition and I'm not sure if it is still making more sense.
It's like looking at twins from a rear view mirror.

The Treasury Department is responsible for: formulating and recommending economic financial, tax *and fiscal policies*; serving as a financial agent for the U.S. Government, protecting the integrity of the financial system and manage the U.S. government finances and resources. It is responsible for auctions, Bonds and Securities, coins currency, foreign transactions, licensing and reporting fraud, waste, abuse, taxes and treasury payments.
The Federal Reserve Board provides a detailed look at the structure, responsibilities and operations of the Federal Reserve System. Incorporation major changes in the law and the structure of the financial system in the past decade.
1-Overview of the FRS 2 –Monetary policy & the economy 3-The implementation of *Monetary policy* 4- The Federal Reserve in the International sphere 5- Supervision & regulation 6-Consumer and community affairs 7-The FR in the U.S. payment System.
(Sources: Both have individual sites on the net.)

Now that it is all clear like mud, we can go on and try to understand the buying and selling of Treasury Bonds between the two.

In a recent article, March 17 2011, by Caroline Salas is questioning Mr. Bernanke on his Quantitative Easing (QE2) policy for Bloomberg, Bernanke proves to his worst critic, Ron Paul, that QE2 is working and it is not contributing to inflation or hyperinflation.

To begin with, most analysts were worried that after or during the recession we were going to experience deflation and then stagflation. With an acceptable price increase of 1.6% to 2.0%, things seem to be under control since the stock market and the Bond market are up (18% for stocks) since last August 27. The risk premium for 10 year Bond is 5.16% from 6.81%.

In my book, people invest in stocks for fighting inflation and not to be contented with a stagnant return on their taxable investments. In other words, people or investors were expecting inflation. Inflation is better than deflation and stagflation. It means that things are moving and there is some economic activity. It's almost like, ''good cholesterol''. We need a little fat in our veins so as inflation.

Unemployment went to 8.9% from 9.0% to Bernanke's enjoyments.

The junk Bond market is humming at a $72.9 billion of borrowing and bank asset ballooned to $2.56 trillion and the Bank rate is still close to zero.

The Government reserve rate could be increased and the consumer's credit could be tightened if needed.

So far, QE2 seemed to be working and everything is under control from the captain's chair point of view.

My concern is this new money created and transferred through OPEN MARKET OPERATIONS is done to give better lending leverage to consumers so that they can go out and buy houses and other durable goods? If the banks use this extra money to speculate in the stock market and commodities' the consumer is not better off. It is the bank lending policy that dictates how much is going into the system to spur back the economy. If the banks don't want to lend, all this extra money won't do much good. One proof of this is that the stock market is up since then and unemployment is still at 9.1%. The money is going into the financial system but not in the real economy where tangible investments are needed in order to create jobs.

As I mentioned before as far is the National debt is concerned, most people think the government can get away with it by simply printing money and that is it or if the debt is too large with other countries and the IMF, then reschedule at a lower rate and then are afoot again.
I'm restating this view because it sounds a bit sarcastic and simple but it is the truth.
In a study from Peterson for International Economics by Joseph Gagnon about countries Sovereign debt comes without a conclusion where the maximum of debt is acceptable measure as a percentage of GDP. Now the US, is at 67% external debt (excluding intra-governmental debt) of GDP and some European countries are much higher as much as over 100% of GDP. Italy, Belgium Japan, Portugal and Spain. Greece presently is at 157.7% of GDP.
As we can assume is that too much payment on debt will hinder economic growth by simply looking at the transfer of money allocating to service the debt that won't go into the economy or social programs. Too much debt would also put the government in a bind to borrow at reasonable rates or being able to borrow at all. *This is the apex of the borrowing.* The solution lies on the level of interest rates, where you want on the one hand create savings, which is interesting for household in order that ''household'' can buy government

debt and not too high a percentage to choke economic growth of the high cost of money.

This seems to be a ''one wrench fix'' for the economy.

Before cutting spending and rising taxes, this is the only way to monitor the economy as long as the population's age is young enough to pay taxes and not receiving a pension check from governments.

Aging seems to be more rapid in Europe as opposed to the US, giving them less leeway to increase taxes. Raising taxes become severe until the population becomes disenchanted with governments and walk in the streets to protest. Sounds familiar?

This is the worst case scenario before governments renegotiate debt with longer payments at lower interest rates. As I mentioned before, governments live forever as long as the population lives for ever. We do die but we do have natal replenishment.

Government's borrowing as a cost. The rate it borrows and the conditions attached and to whom it borrows. European countries have a choice to borrow from the ECB, to the European Financial Stability Fund (EFSF) and at the IMF.

It is better to borrow without austerity conditions at a lower rate but by in large, it is a small price to pay for a reasonable rate and accessibility to markets. Portugal's problem is that the economy is stagnant and the outlook for growth is obscurely dim. So, it tries to borrow without losing too many feathers and still look good on the political side.

They can always give some 40 year old Porto wines in collateral.

Greece promised to privatize $ 25 billion in governmental asset to ease of some future borrowing.

If we come back at the US debt which is 97% of GDP (Both foreign and intra-governmental) which in comparison is less severe than some European counterparts, but it is still an overhang because of its size; $ 14.26 trillion.

Looking at an interview with Carmen M. Reinhart from Peterson Institute, she mentioned that this debt is historically high and thus scares people and politician alike. She is more worried about the household level debt and financial institutions debt as oppose to the government's debt and contingent liabilities of government like Social Security and Medicare. (65 trillions)

It does make sense for the US is a market economy, meaning that household spending will get the economy moving. The recovery is slow, since its' unemployment is still high and borrowing ratio is still high since assets have depleted by more than 30%. Savings relative to income is growing but it is money not spent in the economy.

By in large, the economy will get the debt down when it gets going or a rise in corporate tax and cutting on government spending is eminent. As of today, April 14, 2011, the Obama's administration has decided to cut spending and raise taxes. They want to make sure the next Bond auction goes well at a reasonable yield.

So there is manoeuvre in tweaking the economy and make things credible and bracing, that consumers will bail the economy out of its lagging performance.

APRIL 16-2011 **DEAD RECKONING (DR)**
Legislating a ceiling maximum for the deficit of $14.3 trillion without taking concrete action is more or less like buying a new shirt and a new tie and ticking that people will believe you got a new suit. It is just window dressing.

But since, without mixing the two actions, Obama spoke of reducing the deficit by $4.0 trillion in the next twelve years by raising taxes and limiting spending.

The markets responded well. The 10 year note closed at a yield of 3.47% the lowest in ten years.

The same ten year note yield 6.92% in 1980 and 5.48% from 1998 to 2001.

APRIL 23-2011

It seems like the warning by the Standard & Poor's Bond rating services didn't affect bond yields. On the contrary the yields have declined. The 2 year note yield is 0.66% and the 10 year note went to 3.40% yield. (Meaning price went upwards).

A warning is not the same as action but on the other hand, I can't see the rating of the US treasury downgrading which would have a significant effect around the world.

Politicking is part of governments all around the world, meaning that saying what sounds good and what people want to hear. Politicians will give the least bad news to the public and highlighting the good news.

For instance mentioning that inflation is at 2.7% annualized sound pretty good and reasonable while food and gas and oil are increasing over 35% in the past 6 months. That, what makes people annoyed by the reality and their shrinking purchasing power.

If you take the devaluation of the US dollar into account, what it had lost on the exchange towards other currencies, it surpasses by a mile the 2.7% annual inflation stated since the dollar depreciated 15% against the Euro in the last year and a half.

^USDEUR - U.S. Dollar/Euro FX (FOREX) - Daily OHLC Chart
Op:0.69604, Hi:0.69649, Lo:0.68256, Cl:0.69370

Fruits and vegetables rose by 4.7% just last month. Coffee by 3.5%. Fuel Oil by 37.2 % in the last six months. The Food Index rose at 2.7% just in the last 3 months, how can it be the same for the year? It means more like 12% and predicted to increase by 7.8% in 2011.

Someone's slide rule must of slipped to come up with a rate below 3.0% of inflation and the World Bank say it is 3.6% Just look at China increase consumption of arable land to make way for industrialization lost 8.33 million hectares or 20.6 million acres of farming capacity in the last 12 years, which will turn out as imports on the world market.

Corn, wheat and soybeans never have been so high.   (See monthly tabulations)

Why pretend that inflation is under control? Holding off on the rise of interest rates in case it chokes the economy?

Some commodity experts say that the world is producing just what it consumes as far as agricultural commodities. A little scary when one thinks about the population growth, doesn't it? No one wants to pay 50% of their disposable income on food and the rest on housing.

GLOBALIZATION! DID IT WORK?

GLOBALIZATION was seen as the way out for undeveloped countries and benefiting every single country at the same time. A premise that sounded logical, get more benefit by trade around the world, thus every one participating would rise even salvaged.

Based on the GATT of the 1947 agreement, the WTO was created in 1995 with 153 members to alleviate protectionist and have all its members benefit from free trade and served as a multilateral agreement.

In other words, all countries were competing in a world market thus generating more export for every one of its members.

How come some African countries are still acutely poor?

How come governments are on the bricks not being able to cover their debt payment?

How come the US Government managed the have a record $14.0 trillion deficit?

With the naked eye, I can see that the rich are *getting richer and the poor are getting poorer.*

They are more billionaire popping up everywhere; Russia, China, Mexico, India and the US.

Why does it seem so easy for some and on the same token, people are rioting around the world for almost anything showing their discontent. People think they are not getting their fair share and certainly African countries are dire straight, still facing sickness and extreme poverty. How come Malaria, HIV and AIDS and the lack of drinkable water are still present if we are doing so well and we are still not immune from a global recession of happening one more time. *Answer: Cleavage in societies, cleavage in income, cleavage in education and cleavage in health care and general '' well-being.''*

People want things to be better for them and for their children which are not measured in income or GDP.
Better health care
Better education system and more accessible
Price stability on food and housing
For more equitable salaries for teachers
Less speculation on real estate and stock and commodity markets
Less pollution from automobiles and trucks which should run on propane gas
Less frivolous spending on wars and more equal distribution of wealth.
In other words: The choice between guns or butter. An old economic dilemma when our society should have a say in all crucial decision making.

What seems obvious who benefited from Globalization are the International Corporations. Sure it benefited the small ones, the ones that can export anywhere by just holding an Internet site but the larger companies have gained so much power that they do call the shots even over governments. *They are undeniably the bullies on the street.*
Large Corporations have created a large surface retail outlets which made the corner store impossible to compete with large offering and unbeatable prices, out-wiping the corner store and the small strip mall of yesterday; Economies of scale at its finest.

Large Corporations can bribe governments by possible ''job creation'' by obtaining subsidies, grants, tax relief and reduced or lenient pollution laws while their executives live like kings. They are flexible, able to move anywhere where labour is cheap, where taxes are less or non -existent, where technology is available and governments are open and research laws are lax and clinical trials of any sort encouraged. Every governments will been over backward to have jobs to offer their electoral constituency.

This why manufacturing shifted to lesser expensive labor countries at the expense of the US labor where the service industry and communication companies now prevails like Google and Microsoft, Yahoo and Cisco and Facebook and so on.

Globalization has seemed to help the 2008-09-10 recession by accentuating the rapidity of financial institutions around the world of taking a beating on their investments with their CDO's. (*Collaterized Debt Obligation*). In other words, they are package of debt, mainly mortgages of different quality of sub-prime debt which demands a higher yield. Most often, the yield is 2 to 3 % higher than regular corporate bonds. CDO is basically ''created bonds'' which comprise of mortgages part of what they call:'' Synthetic Security Market''

It created facility for US financial institutions to sell mortgages (CDO) packages to institutions to foreign banks and mutual funds and pension funds around the world. Not that product itself is bad, but merchant banks could sell those to other banks or financial institutions without changing their balance sheets. In other words, they remained on the books as asset while they re-sold them and didn't have the protection needed or capital requirement set by law. The other failure was the rating agencies didn't have the knowhow to assess the CDO because they were many qualities of mortgages, so they rated them AAA , qualifying legal investments for pension funds and insurance companies, which was not the case. When one could obtain a mortgage with 5% down, it was easy to become a homeowner even if you didn't qualify. The mortgage industry blew the walls of common sense, lending to people with hardly any income and people went to buy houses they couldn't afford.

And the balloon kept on growing based on air.

Technology helped the creation of Derivatives and CDO and made it available to speculators around the world, so that obscene speculation can take place. Globalization has made it easier to sell them around the world. The worst of all, things got so complex and with a rapidity that government regulators were surpassed by it all and decided not to regulate Derivatives and CDO's.

Derivatives are future contract with an underlying security. A good hedger if you are a farmer or a buyer of the underlying commodity or asset, but purely speculative if you are not.

You're betting a premium that you can lose completely.

They even invented ''Weather Derivatives.'' Kind of difficult to get hold of the weather don't you think?

(See Wikipedia on Derivatives and CDO if you want to more)

Even rating organizations like Standard & Poor's, or Moody's were overwhelmed by the bigness of growing market and complexity of the new products and how it affected the balance sheet of US banks, and were caught by rating these financial institutions AAA rating days before their collapse just based on their fast growing, but ''empty'' asset base.

I won't try to summarize the financial meltdown that occurred on Wall Street because some have done a good job of deciphering this ''can of worms'' like Charles Fergusson with his film; *INSIDE JOB* and Charles Morris with his book; *THE TWO TRILION DOLLAR MELTDOWN* and Mr. N. Roubini in his book; *CRISIS ECONIMICS*. One thing I can do is trying to understand why it came to such a financial disaster and took all other financial institutions with them and created the biggest world recession we ever experienced since 1929.

I'm afraid that two things which are overlooked in the capitalistic system which his *greed* and *crime*.

They are well recognized after the fact but never before.

If we look closely before every recession we had in North America excessive speculation and white collar crime was present. Even the ''dot-com bubble'' was infiltrated with lies and false researched documentations and easy access to broker's capital (private investors) with shears promises and an unknown territory for most. We were beguiled by salesman and their ''snake oil talk'' which we couldn't fully understand.

Those two factors are difficult to notice because they are part of the human North American psychic and very difficult to assess when occurring but present until the bubble explodes.

History has to be of some use here, for us to learn a lesson but we seem to never do until we create bubbles by excess speculation and fraud and then we burst.

Regulatory organizations never seem to be able to catch up until it is too late. Allen Greenspan, chairman of the Federal Reserve Board never saw it coming. PhD in Economics, ex-professor, government employee for numerous years, adviser to the president, never saw it coming? How can the layman see it coming?

The saying ''greed is good, a lack of a better word'' for the economy like the character Greco said in the film Wall Street interpreted by Michael Douglass, is a statement that needs reflection.

Prosperity is good (which is a better word) until massive speculation occurs and fraud and then it BURST.

Globalization did help the financial sector to collapse in a matter of weeks, taking the real economy down with it.

NO VALUE is created by adding premiums to assets. It is simply adding to the risk.

In order to put a positive recommendation on this is to have more regulations on financial transactions and not let brokers and bankers govern the world by creating instruments that don't make economic sense like Derivatives and CDO's. Rounding up a bunch of mortgages that then selling them two to three or four times and try to ask the house owner if the payments are coming. Even now after the big mess, 2011, financial and mortgage companies are in baffling predicament to retrace the legal papers of repossessed houses because things went so fast and documents that needed to be signed and delivered were simply not. Some legal papers were forged to expedite things. Time is money!

What kind of a web we weave?

GOVERNMENTAL STATISTICS

Ever since I've studied economics, 45 years ago, most of the government reporting seems to be the same and did lose some credibility among analyst about the reality of the numbers released.

As I mentioned before, the core CPI is not representative of the real inflation rate since two years now when it *excluded* the Food section and the Energy section.

The unemployment figure released since two years or so of 9% in the US is not believed by people and most think it is a much larger percentage.

Even the percentage of inflation released by China of 5% is not believed by followers of economics and most believe that China has an inflation rate of 10%.

His that constellation of figures is really serving something useful? I most believe they are wrong and they are used to make policies which are wasteful and misleading.

Academic economists are taking a good view on how statistics are published and are skeptical about the most watched statistic, the GDP. Getting out of recession is a concern for all countries and everyone is monitoring their economic growth. Even with good growth figures, people wonder why they are not getting better lives.

The rich are getting richer and the poor are getting poorer. Sounds familiar?

Obviously, the gap between the two groups is widening and does give a false sense of well- being based on a non-representation of the average.

''Average'' is the most misleading word in economic reports. If my statement is true, that the rich are getting richer and the poor are getting poorer, the ''average'' is getting worse off. The other element which is misleading is that economic growth or GDP is not representative of ''well-being.'' Nicolas Sarkozy sponsored a commission to evaluate the way Government use reporting and particularly the measure of economic growth for all countries. Mr. Joseph E. Stiglitz after he was employed by the World Bank, made some recommendations to the French government based on how we can measure our lives besides using the standard GDP.

Remember when we were teens that our mother told us that money isn't happiness and love could not be bought?

It is true that the well-being of people is difficult to measure since it does not solely depend on expenditures and the standard of living. This brings us to the quality of life which is not taken into account like; condition of health, the level of activity, social blending, quality air, availability of services like medical, utilities and clean water. Not to mention love and freedom and security which are essential to well-being. Those are present or absent regardless of your income and expenditure.

Some economists came forward with new ways of compiling well-being beside the regular GDP.

Is it the GNH, Gross General Happiness, put forward by Mr. Bhutan and the ISEW, the Index of Sustainable Economic Welfare or the GPI, the Genuine Progress Indicator created by Nordhaus & Tobin, we should be looking at for the future? The GDP doesn't look at the footprint we leave on the environment and certainly doesn't come up with the actual or long term cost. The GDP doesn't measure if this ''growth'' is sustainable or not and how much we use of non-reusable resources and how much this contributes to real wealth and not some passing ephemeral binge on nature.

I have yet to see from any Government declare a five and ten year plan to create real wealth for its citizens. Presently, we are running after energy; where? How much? And at what cost? Ever since we realized that the production of energy is equal to consumption, we are in a dire straight to be self-sufficient. In other words, we want to cover our ass in regards to energy dependency. This is the long term plan.

In the last twenty years or so, the service industry as has grown rapidly at the expense of exporting manual jobs overseas, led by the communication industry. Now that our cars and TV and all labor intensive product are made in China, Korea and India, we are concentrating on making widgets, the kind of communication tools that are fun, exciting and fashionable. But how much wealth does it represent for a nation when these widgets are easily surpassed by innovation by the companies who made them and become almost obsolete in one year.

There are mountains of obsolete cell phones, computers and television sets accumulating in India and soon I Pods and other Tablets, because it is the only country that will accept garbage

in mass quantity since they are so poor and they are trying to rescue any precious metal they can find in them.
Is that accumulating WEALTH or producing more garbage?

Education is another commodity which is difficult to measure at looking at the GDP. How much of a figure you put on education or degrees now that lots of engineers and M.B.A's are looking for jobs and have accumulated enormous debts with their student loans paying strangulating college fees that runs in the tenth of thousands?
How do you measure IMMIGRATION? Tertiary jobs or illegal immigrants that are needed to do the job we don't want to do? Do we calculate human capital only if they're educated? The problem of computing statistics is challenging to say the least and more so how to interpret them and make some assumptions and create government policies.
My only answer since statistics have to be taken with a grain of salt, or two, we have to look at our happiness before our consumption level.

GOVERNMENTAL RESPOSIBILITIES

With the freedom we all have in our capitalist system is that we can speculate to make profits as much as we like as long as it is legal. The Governments (Fed & States) are the watchdogs through its multiple agencies.
The one thing our system is afraid of is ''inflation'' which they are not too many tools available to control it. What inflation led to is a bursting bubble like we seen in the past so many times, where everything comes crashing down. A Boom and Bust economy.

When we fall into a recession, we are a shame that greed got over us, one more time and now we have to repent for years and reflect on what we did wrong.

If inflation is enemy number one; speculation is the fuel behind it which creates uncontrollable fire. WALL STREET is like a seven year old kid with a loaded gun. It thinks of speculation, it dreams of speculation. Where the money comes from? From investors, from the common people: from you. These financial wizards spent sleepless nights trying to come up with a new device to literally screw people or what they call; *transferring the risk* to the sappy.

When they create devices to attract people, they make it complicated so that people will say; if I can't understand it, it must genial.

We all saw what "bundle Mortgage back Securities" ended up; defunct bonds.

Now they are thinking of bundling Life Insurance policies, make a package and then sell them at a higher price with the mirage of substantial returns. Like the headlines said: *Wall Street wants you to die.*

We all do but if you die sooner than later, the payoff is quicker.

Why is it that Governmental agencies don't regulate these "Creative Bonds" and applies strict guidelines or disapprove them all together before they come to market?
Because they think if "they "are smart enough to come up with this, it must be good.

WRONG.

Only greed made them do it. Not only greed and sell the package to more greedy people, they are getting rid of the risk while making a commission.

Easy speculation environment is the breeding ground for FRAUD.

I don't think crooks get into Wall Streets but when cash is so easily available and lots of it, in the hundreds of millions, greedy people get the ''Dr. Jekyll and Mr. Hyde'' effect. They turn on you from being your best admonitory friend to a devilish advocate of greed.

How much speculation goes into the GSCI? (Goldman Sachs Commodity Index-1991)
the commodity index that is available for speculation and responsible for high price on commodities? One fifth of all trades are pure speculators as oppose to hedgers; literally the buyers and the sellers of the underlying commodities. That is 20% of traders are there to make profits, and of course pushing prices upward.
Shouldn't the regulatory bodies step in?
Nobody likes paying more for food, nobody.

ON GOLD

Gold prices are getting suspiciously interesting since it is not going down and carries silver (the poor men's gold) along with it. Without baring any interest or dividend or cash flow, people think they are better off with precious metals rather than currency. On one hand, currencies are fiat money, not based on real value since the gold standard has been abolished, but gold has a Philistine connotation to it. You can't eat it, you can't give it to the grocery store, and it doesn't bare any dividends either and most of all, as no intrinsic value.
China with the $3 trillion holdings in reserve in US dollar is thinking of converting 1 trillion in gold. That will surely increase the price to the roof, and there isn't any roof.
China wants the world to use the Yuan as currency and if it does buy the gold, it would probably be more than what the US Government is holding. The US is holding 8,134 tonnes of it, being the biggest holder in the world. On a *per capita* basis,

the US comes *ten* in rank and the first is Switzerland with 1,040 tonnes. (Source: The Economist)

I believe that per capita basis is significant since the Swiss Franc is quite strong against the US dollar and other currencies.

I think this battle of currencies might end if governments agree to go back at the table and negotiate a *gold standard* related US dollar like it was before in 1971 since people like gold more than currencies. Creating the EURO might have been a precursor of it, unifying money in a more global sense and get away from daily exchanges.

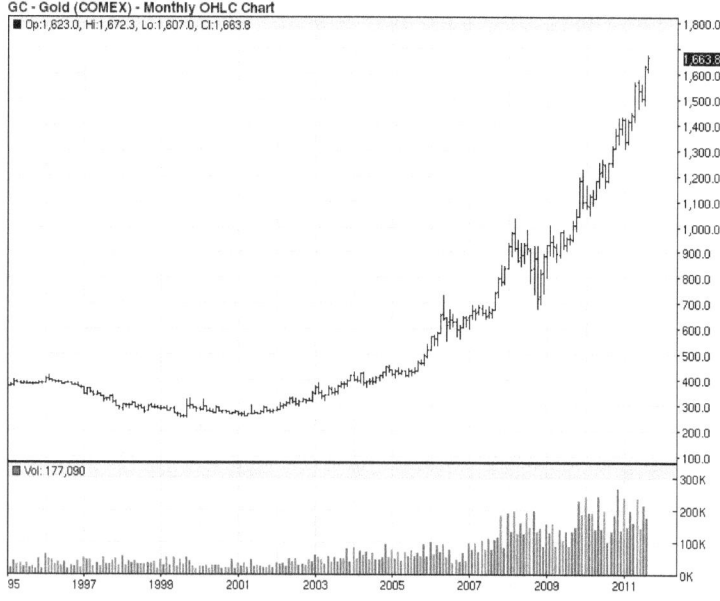

GC - Gold (COMEX) - Monthly OHLC Chart

There were talks and papers written on the possibility to join the US dollar, the Canadian dollar and the Mexican pesos to form a single currency, the three countries of North America. I think the talks were on one side only.

In my daily comments about the news and it false premises and reactions, gold comes up often as a subject since there have been a substantial increase in its price and silver even more so. It is a daily quotation by people in the investment game that the UD dollar is going down and the precious metal is going up. As I mentioned before since people favour gold more than the USD, why not go back to the pegging of gold on USD. It was done before and could be done again.

Utah as issued the Legal Tender Act means that people can convert gold and silver for dollars on collateral borrowing for business transactions. Sounds like a step towards pegging gold to the greenback. Other States are in the process of doing so as well. Some European countries have the subject on the table. I'm sure in a couple of years, gold will be tied to currencies somehow since all the European banking system is due for a reorganization and the IMF is working overtime to make sense of country's debt and the World Bank trying to come up with a formula to stabilize currencies and stopping its havoc.

Bretton Woods Agreement III?

EPILOGUE

As the world turns, quoting a name of a TV program of many years ago, I wanted to highlight in this book the exaggerated control of international companies on prices of commodities and how much price increase is often the results of political crisis around the world which are exogenous to real supply and is the base of exploitation by large firms and speculators increasing their profits at the expense of consumers.

I think I have reached that point where commodity prices were at their peak when political turmoil was at its peak in the Middle East and some climate change news occurred influencing prices more drastically without really quantifying its effect.

Wars and droughts and flood due influence commodity market prices *without any doubts* thinking that supply could be interrupted and shortage will occur and high prices follows, worrying consumers that things are going to get more expensive along the line.

In all commodities they are reserves to be used when annual crops failed to match demand due to shortage for any reason. When reserves are used, this is when prices go up dramatically on a given day thinking that we just might run out. Reserves are at lower cost than current cost but they are selling reserves at higher prices. It happened in crude oil and corn and in wheat. The percentage of the depletion of reserves wasn't mentioned and it was left to the media to leave consumers worried about the future.

First, reserves are there for the adjustment of failing crops since it does happen from time to time that nature doesn't cooperate, the intrinsic risk of agriculture.

Secondly, most reserves of agricultural products are perishable and thus it is not savvy to accumulate large reserves just in case of catastrophic results. Production on most agricultural commodities is one step ahead of demand but not two or three steps ahead. Even in crude oil production, we have reserve but we are close to the demand in a given year. We have a large surplus in recession times but by in large, we consume very close to what we produce.

Giving the fact that China economic growth is constantly in the double digits and emerging countries like India and Brazil are showing exceptional growth as well are factors which makes demand for all products unpredictable but *newsworthy* to exploit by raising prices.

It is at times, and I admit, worrisome, thinking that oil and agricultural products are so close since those commodities are so crucial for our survival but, yes there is a but, the News have a way to amplify situations with actual fact unchecked. What will be the actual damage and what are the reserves in a giving day when the weather is influencing crops? No one knows
but prices do go up dramatically in a single day.

My point was also proven in regards to oil, when political unrest existed in the Middle East when the perception of running out of oil and the increases in gasoline in North America was simply unjustified since a shortage of supply never been a threat.

The consumer is given the royal finger by multinational corporations and speculators creating hype from crisis and collecting high profits by pushing prices spontaneously.

The long awaited news of August the second was indeed a crucial moment in US history when an agreement between the Republicans and the Democrats had to be reach until the last day to raise the debt ceiling in order to pay its debt on foreign and domestic bonds and its contingent liabilities. It did create uncertainties among the world but there was no way that Republicans would have forgone the obligations of the United States.

The other major factors investors of US Bonds were concerned about was the rating by agencies of the quality of the US treasury bonds from AAA to AA+, which did happen on August 5 after market close. The following Monday August 8, stock market reacted negatively by losing 3% a day two days in a row but also it confirmed that the US was indeed in trouble since the last quarter growth of GDP was only 1.3% annualized.

One thing which was a concern expressed by specialists was how much is the amount of speculation there is in the commodity futures' market? Since the commodities' market followed the stock market decline, *it does confirm that there is a lot of speculative money* in the agricultural commodities' market compared with hedgers.

I have to say that these rapid declines confirmed my premise that prices are influenced by the News and by speculation even in agricultural commodities.

Where were the droughts, where were the floods, where was the possibility of reduced supply on any commodities in those days? Nowhere!

Only cotton managed to go up on bad crops due to droughts in Texas. But again, I didn't hear that there was a shortage of ''shirts and pants'' in any country. Who is on a kitting binge?

It is evident that markets are a reflection of things to come, but only a reflection valued by the psychic of speculators and influences the spot markets and retail prices for consumers. The high gas retail prices are a perfect example of how the price was controlled by large companies based on making believe that the shortage was imminent and they remained

high to this day when the WTI has fallen considerably from its high.
Since the US economy is so lethargic, 1.3% growth, gas prices should be at the bottom not at their highest, since it is the largest consumer of oil. When good economic news is published, the prices of crude oil due go up, why not down when the news is dismal?

Conclusion:
I'm afraid that we need more Governmental control and new policies and regulations in the banking industry and futures market and in all markets. I think that fund managers and traders should be personally liable for losses occurred to others and remunerations should not be based on performance and the number of trades, where a conflict of interest lies. Speculation is an inward reaction of greed and present in mankind since the days of dawn.

END

ECONOMIC SYSTEMS EXPLAINED.

Since some people have difficulty understanding economic systems, since they are different in most countries, I thought I would explain it in a simpler fashion;

SOCIALISM
You have two cows. You give one to your neighbour.

COMMUNISIM
You have two cows. The State takes both and gives you some milk.

FACISM
You have two cows. The State takes both and sells you the milk.

NAZISM
You have two cows. The States takes both and shoots you.

BUREAUCRATISM
You have two cows. The State takes both, shoots one, milk the other, and then throws the milk away.

TRADITIONAL CAPITALIST
You have two cows. You sell one and buy a bull. Your herd multiplies, and the economy grows. You sell them and retire on the income.

AN AMERICAN CORPORATION
You have two cows. You sell one, and force the other to produce the milk of four cows. Later, you hire a consultant to analyze why the cow has dropped dead.

VENTURE CAPITALISM
You have two cows. You sell three of them to your publicly listed company using a letter of credit opened by your brother in law at the bank, to execute a debt/equity swap with an associated general offer so that you can get four cows back, with a tax exemption for your wife cows. The milk rights of

the six cows are transferred via an intermediate to a Cayman Island Company secretly owned by the majority shareholders who sells the right to all seven cows back to your listed company. The annual report says the company owns eight cows, with an option on one more. You sell one cow to buy a new president, leaving you with nine cows. No balance sheet provided with the release. The public then buys your bull. (Source unknown)

APPENDIX OF COMMODITY PRICES-MONTHLY MOVEMENTS

Feb.04-March-04-April-May-June-July-

ENERGY

Brent Crude Future (USD/bbl.)
100.180--114.98—121.03—125.99--115.84-114.39
Gas Oil Future (ICE) (USD/MT)
848.750-- 958.5—1,008.75—1,040.00-953.75-941.25
Heating Oil Future(USD/gal.)
272.030-- 303.8—316.22—327.85-305.67-298.61
Natural Gas Future (USD/MM.Btu)
4.318---3.80— 4.28— 4.709---4.707---4.374
Gasoline RBOB Future USD/gal.)
244.600--299.04—315.88--- 340.120-299.310-301.2
WTI Crude Future (USD/bbl.)
89.50-- 100.92—108.310---114.27—100.22--97.34

AGRICULTURAL

Canola Future (WCE) (CAD3MT)
607.700--593.80—581.50---570.90—599.80-555.90
Cocoa Future-LI (GBP/MT)
2,150.00—2,374.0—1,955.00-1,981.00-1,779.0-2023.
Cocoa Future(USd/MT)
3,282.00-- 3716.0—3,020.00—3,280.0-2,878.0-3,228
Coffee ''C'' Future(USd/lb.)
249.450--271.5—256.05---306.75—270.95-269.15
Corn Future(USD/Bu
666.270--724.5—760.250—747.00--754.0---607.0
Cotton no.2 Future (USD/lb.)
168.270--203.11—195.55—154.210-138.78—115.25
FCOJ-A-Future(USD/lb.)
172.600--177.00—165.200-171.200-181.90-186.90
Wheat Future (CBT)USD/Bu
853.750--818.75—790.00—803.250-773.75-633.75
Wheat Future (KCB) (USD/Bu)

943.00—915.0—958.500—899.500-914.250-739.50
Sugar #11 (world) (USD/lb.)
32.840—30.02—25.93---21.68---23.95---27.65
Soybean Future(USD/Bu)
1,431.00-1,396.25-1,384.00-1,388.75-1,414.50-1313.5
Lumber Future ($/1,000 board ft.)
300.90--305.40—314.60---258.90-227.0-262.0
Oat Future (USD/Bu)
414.450—392.0-394.00—348.75—378.0355.75
Rough Rice (CBOT) (USDcwt.)
16.185—14.25—13.915—15.205-14.475-15.255
Soybean-meal. Future (USD/lb.)
383.20—366.60—357.0—360.50-368.40-339.5
Soybean Oil Future (USD/lb.)
58.98—58.65—58.88 ----58.60—58.73—56.34
Wool Future (SFE) (cents/kg.)
1,175.000-1180.0-1,307.00-264.00-1,429.0-1,475.0
INDUSTRIAL METALS
Copper Future(USD/lb.)
460.400-452.65-425.200-418.200-413.45-434.6
PRECIOUS METALS
Gold 100 oz. Future(USD/t.oz.)
1,348.80-1427.9-1,435.1-1,569.700-1542.40-1,512.9
Silver Future (USD/t.oz.)
28.93----34.58—--38.59---- 46.89---36.19-35.45
LIVESTOCK
Live Cattle Future(USD/lb.)
112.925-113.05-120.85---112.80-105.100-113.4
Cattle Feeder Future(USD/lb.)
125.100-133.70-141.55-135.325-124.25-141.55
Lean Hogs Future(USD/lb.)
91.300—88.42—104.025---95.60—87.85-93.20
 Source: Bloomberg-Commodity Futures Online.

The major increases during the month of February, the month of the bedlam in Egypt and Libya was the WTI index of 16% and Brent Oil F index of 15% and Oil &Gas F of 12,9% coffee 8.5%, gold of 6% and silver of 20%.

I can understand more the precious metals increase, a refuge from inflated currencies but North American oil prices (WTI) are simply manifestations of being scared of scarcity.

''The only thing we have to fear is fear itself.'' Franklin D. Roosevelt.

As I mentioned before.

Retail gas prices (reg. average) is $3.509 US gal. (03/05-2011)

$3.368 a week ago

$3.122 a month ago.

$2.747 a year ago.

Source: Fuel gage report.com

and Canadian prices are 139.7 cents/ litre (reg.av) as of 03/06-2011)

Source: Gasticker.com.

APPENDIX OF COMMODITY PRICES-MONTHLY MOVEMENTS

August 3-

ENERGY

Brent Crude Future (USD/bbl.)	113.87
Gas Oil Future (ICE) (USD/MT)	955.75
Heating Oil Future(USD/gal.)	304.210
Natural Gas Future (USD/MMBtu)	4.093
Gasoline RBOB Future USD/gal.)	295.66
WTI Crude Future (USD/bbl.)	92.28

AGRICULTURAL

Canola Future (WCE) (CAD3MT)	567.0
Cocoa Future-LI (GBP/MT)	1,842.0
Cocoa Future (USD/MT)	2,921.0
Coffee ''C'' Future(USd/lb.)	242.50

Corn Future(USd/Bu	708.500
Cotton no.2 Future (USd/lb.)	105.100
FCOJ-A-Future(USd/lb.)	199.85
Wheat Future (CBT)USd/Bu)	746.75
Wheat Future (KCB) (USd/Bu)	793.25
Sugar #11 (world) (USd/lb.)	27.88
Soybean Future(USd/Bu)	1,370.50
Lumber Future ($/1,000 board ft.)	223.40
Oat Future (USD/Bu)	356.25
Rough Rice (CBOT) (USDcwt.)	16.285
Soybean-meal. Future (USD/lb.)	360.20
Soybean Oil Future (USD/lb.)	57.48
Wool Future (SFE) (cents/kg.)	1,376.00
INDUSTRIAL METALS	
Copper Future(USD/lb.)	433.50
PRECIOUS METALS	
Gold 100 oz. Future(USD/t.oz.)	1,670.80
Silver Future (USD/t.oz.)	41.675
LIVESTOCK	
Live Cattle Future(USD/lb.)	117.525
Cattle Feeder Future(USd/lb.)	135.0
Lean Hogs Future(USd/lb.)	91.250

Source: Bloomberg-Commodity Futures Online.

Suggested Readings (books):

Milton Friedman & Anna Schwartz. *A Monetary History of the United States 1867-1960*
Robert Bryce. *Gusher of lies: Dangerous Delusions of Energy Independence*.

Milton Friedman. *Capitalism and Freedom*

Ralph Nader. *Only the Super Rich Can Save Us*.

William Black. *The Best way to Rob a bank is to Own One*.

Karl Webber. *Food Inc.*

Katrina Vanden Heuvel. *Meltdown*

Tom Bower. *Oil: Money Politics and Power*

John Hofmeister. *Why we hate the Oil companies*

Brian Sussman. *Climategate (Global warming scam)*

Joel Balkan. *The Corporation*

Naomi Klein. *The Shock Doctrine*

Naomi Klein. *No LOGO*

Noam Chomsky. Many books

Edwin Black. *IBM and the Holocaust*

Michel Chossudovshy. *The Globalization of poverty (CGR)*

Peter Tertzakian. *The End of Obesity Energy*

The Day the Dollar Die

Umair Hague. *The New Capitalist Manifesto*

James Buchanan. *The New Public Choice Theory*

Russel Napier. *Anatomy of the Bears-Learning from Wall's street four great Bottoms*

Charles Ferguson. *Inside Job*. Film-documentary

John Ralston Saul. *The Collapse of Globalism*

Charles Norris. *The two Trillion dollar meltdown*

Nourie Roubini. *Crisis Economics, a crash course in the future of finance*

Steven Drobny & Nourie Roubini. *The Invisible Hands: Top hedge fund traders on bubbles, crises, and real money.*

Joseph E. Stiglitz. *Miss-measuring our lives. Why GDP doesn't add up.*

Boris, Jean Pierre. *Le Roman Noir des Matières Premières*

Tyler Cowen. *The Great Stagnation*

Robyn O'Brien. *The power of one*

Consumer magazines:

Consumers Report-Consumers Digest-Choice magazine-
Which (UK) -Ethical Consumers-
Consumer-Organic Authority-Consumer.gov./NCPW
Inflation-food price hikes
Food Navigator USA.

Sites consulted for research Data

EWG.org   Environmental Working Group.

Gurufocus.com Donald Fox

Live Oil Prices.co.uk/oil

USDA.gov

USDE. dept. Of Energy

Topix.com

OANDA.com Forex trading

UNECE. Org United Nations Economics.com

OECD.org Organization for economic co-operation &
development

Eurostat

BEA bureau of economic analysis (US dept. of commerce)

FDA

FIDA

PAM

ONS (UK)

Economics Network. AC. UK for books and tutorials

INDEXMONDI.com

IFM.org

World Bank.org

BLS.gov   (Bureau of labour statistics)

UN.org

Census.gov

Global research.ca (politics)

AMSTAT.org/publications   sub.

Globalinsight.com   subscription.

Consensus Economics.com   Economic forecast-world-historical data

Federal Reserve.gov

Econ Indicator.com

Bank of Canada

Statistics Canada and UK

All business.com

Bureau of investigative Journalist   UK sub.

The false claim Act legal Center.com

Politicol news.com

Healthcare fraud Prevention and Enforcement Action team (HEAT)

Petroleum Economist

Energy Intelligence.com   Weekly letter

PennEnergy.com   (Books available)

C. D. Howe Institute (CDN)

Ecographer.com

Central bank news.com

Trading economics.com (World countries)

Economagic.com   (LIBOR data)

Google Finance.com

Yahoo.finance.com

Global-rates.com (Country's rates)

Food and water watch.org

Organic consumer.org

Coolfood campaign.org

PANNA.org

FIAN.org

Sustainable.org (Agriculture)

GATA.org   Bill Murphy (Gold)

World Oil.com

EIA.doe.gov

WSJ.com

IECD (Development)

Oil.com powered by WN.com

Bloomberg.com

INFOSUD.org

Guardian.co.UK (Newspaper)

NY Times.com

Api.org   (Oil &gas)

The Oil drum.com

Know more.org (Ethical Consumerism)

High Frequency Economics. By Carl Weinberg. Subscription letter.

Grant Interest Rate Observer. By James Grant. Subscription letter.

Dow Jones News Wire Service.

PumpTalk.ca

Conference Board of Canada

M.J. Ervin and Associates

Canadian Center of Energy

Canadian Petroleum Product Institute.com

Fin.gc.ca

Federal Reserve Bank of New York

I I E.com   Peterson Institute for International Economics. Washington, DC

BIS.com   Bank for International Settlements. Switzerland

Lloyd's List Intelligence.com   Tanker's traffic

Hellenic Shipping News.com   Tanker's traffic

Gulf Traffic.com (exhibition-conference) Subscription

Gloom, Boom, Doom Report by Marc Faber   Subscription

Roubini.com Global Economics   Subscription

CRS-Congressional Research Service-Dept. of State

Géopolitis.ch   France

Nickols on gold.com (best)

Markit Economics.com

Agritel.com   France. World market

Baltic Exchange.   Subscription

Milken Institute.org   Conferences

EFSA (Euro Food Safety Authority)

FDIC-(Federal Deposit Insurance Corporation)

WorthWhile.typepad.com   Cdn. Eco.

Waterfootprint.org

CEPR. Net /Index/php/graphic

Fabsites.com   Charts of commodities and currencies.

Gasticker.ca

CME GROUP.COM Acreage report-education/interactive

NYMEX-Commitments of Traders Report

BIOGRAPHY

Mark C. Brown was born in Montreal in 1946, graduated with a B.A in Economics with an Honor's degree from Bishop's University in Lennoxville, Quebec.
He spent most of his career in the investment field as a retail stockbroker (25 years) for various firms in Montreal and spent five years as a real estate broker in the ICI division.
The last five years of his working career was spent as an English teacher of secondary language (TESOL) at home and abroad.
After publishing two basic books in French in 1982-87 on the Stock market and Security investments, he published in 2010 a book on weight management(Set your mind to lose weight for ever) with Publish America and a comparative social study of Americans' eating habits (America on the Scale) with the same publisher in 2011.
Pursuing writing in retirement, The Invisible Finger: How the little guy gets screwed by big Corporations, is his most opinionated work writing on Globalisation and power of corporations.

www.ingramcontent.com/pod-product-compliance
Lightning Source LLC
Chambersburg PA
CBHW071405170526
45165CB00001B/186